Social Reality and Tradition

Social Reality and Tradition

Essays in Modes of Understanding

EDITED BY
BIJOY H. BORUAH
RAMASHANKER MISRA

RAWAT PUBLICATIONS
Jaipur · New Delhi · Bangalore · Mumbai · Hyderabad

ISBN 81-316-0040-8

Published by
Prem Rawat for **Rawat Publications**
Satyam Apts., Sector 3, Jawahar Nagar, Jaipur 302 004 (India)
Phone: 0141 265 1748 / 7006 Fax: 0141 265 1748
E-mail: info@rawatbooks.com
Website: www.rawatbooks.com

New Delhi Office
4858/24, Ansari Road, Daryaganj, New Delhi 110 002
Phone: 011-23263290

Also at Bangalore, Mumbai and Hyderabad

Typeset by Rawat Computers, Jaipur
Printed at Chaman Enterprises, New Delhi

Contents

Acknowledgements

Since this book owes its origin to a national workshop on "The Idea of Human Sciences," held in the Indian Institute of Technology, Kanpur under the auspices of the Indian Institute of Advanced Study, Shimla, Acknowledgements are due to both these Institutes. We are especially indebted to the members of the Faculty of Humanities and Social Sciences of IIT Kanpur, and to many doctoral students, for their unstinted support and cooperation in conducting the workshop. The participants of the workshop, and the resource persons Professors Rajan Gurukkal, Mohini Mullick, Gurpreet Mahajan and Ram Mohan Rao who made the workshop intellectually exciting, all deserve our hearty-felt acknowledgement. In addition, the book partially owes its origin to a symposium on "Understanding Tradition," held in honor of our esteemed colleague Professor Mohini Mullick, on the eve of her retirement from the Department of HSS, IIT Kanpur. It was a fitting tribute to her retirement, and we sincerely acknowledge the inspiration that she had perpetually provided us, which had eventually triggered the initiation of the symposium. The symposium was contiguous, both temporally and conceptually, with the workshop, for the theme was quite relevant to a judicious understanding of the idea of human sciences. Our special acknowledgements are due to the symposiasts: Professors G.C. Pande, A.K. Saran, K.N. Sharma, Rajan Gurukkal, and Mohini Mullick.

We acknowledge the value and effort of all the contributors of this book, and we hope that they would forgive us for the delay in getting our editorial job done. For various reasons, mostly beyond our control, the delay was inevitable. Finally, our special thanks are due to Mr. Varadarajan for admiringly bearing the onus of proofreading, and to Mr. Rajendra Nigam for typing up the manuscript.

Contributors

Rajeev Bhargava is Professor of Political Science at the University of Delhi.

Bijoy H. Boruah is Professor of Philosophy at the Indian Institute of Technology, Kanpur.

Rajan Gurukkal is Director of School of Social Sciences, Mahatma Gandhi University, Kottayam.

Gurpreet Mahajan is Professor at the Centre for Political Studies, Jawaharlal Nehru University, New Delhi

Ramashanker Misra was Professor of Philosophy at the Indian Institute of Technology, Kanpur.

Mohini Mullick was Professor of Philosophy at the Indian Institute of Technology, Kanpur.

G.C. Pande was Chairman, Indian Institute of Advanced Study, Shimla.

T.V.S. Ramamohan Rao was Professor of Economics at the Indian Institute of Technology, Kanpur.

A.K. Saran was Professor of Sociology, Jodhpur University.

Introduction

BIJOY H. BARUAH AND RAMASHANKER MISRA

Part I
Objectivity in Social Understanding

A systematic understanding of the human world, constituted by events and attitudes infused with intentionality, is expected to be an objective comprehension of human nature and the human situation. Admittedly, there are the so-called human sciences, attempting to be systematic, as any science is supposed to be, about their accounts of human intentional phenomena. These sciences cannot but purport to be objective studies about their subject matter, lest they are discredited otherwise as rhetorics of subjectivity.

To what extent is this purported condition of objectivity actually satisfied in a human or social scientific enterprise? This is a question that at first needs to be examined as regards its pertinence, before even trying to answer it in clear terms. The same question may or may not arise with respect to the natural-scientific enterprise, mainly because methodological standards of objectivity are pretty much well defined in the execution of this enterprise. But the question of objectivity emerges quite naturally because, unlike the object-domain of natural sciences, what the human or social sciences study are not objects or situations of a mind-independent order of reality, since its object-domain is culturally constructed, or constituted by the various outlooks and dispositions of the individual and collective psyche of the human race. Despite this difference, a difference of a quasi-ontological sort, the paradigm of an objective enquiry remains a methodological issue for the legitimacy of the human or social sciences. Thus the problem of objectivity in social enquiry or human studies is more tenuous and complex than what it could be in a natural-scientific enquiry.

The idea of a reflective enquiry into human social phenomena has been subject to varied and often radically opposed methodological perspectives. At the centre stage of this perspectival methodological debate has been the empiricist tradition arguing for the natural-scientific model of investigation as appropriate to the study of human social reality. In this orthodox view, it is held that if an enquiry into social phenomena or the human world is to be objective, it must be in terms of social or human *causes and effects* and the explanation must be brought under general socio-psychological laws. Social phenomena must be conceived and construed as *facts* of the 'objective' social world analogous to the way the natural phenomena are taken to be external and objective facts of the natural world. And, it is alleged, this is what makes this sort of enquiry a social or human *science*.

The 'scientism' of this view at its most extreme finds expression in Skinnerian behaviorism on the one hand, and in Wilsonian sociobiology on the other. Economics provides another important example. For the predominant trend in economics has been scientistic of the extreme form, in so far as most economists conceive of economic phenomena, not as irreducibly social phenomena, but as natural ones. And the same trend is noticeable in what has in recent years emerged as 'cognitive science', wherein an understanding of the phenomena of human cognition is sought to be achieved in terms of artificial computational systems.

The underlying belief in all this is that there is an objective fact of the social matter that can be unearthed only by the application of natural-scientific methods and concepts. This, in turn, has the consequence of treating social human reality as if it were merely natural-physical reality. The implied reductionism of the social-human to the natural-physical should mean that human sciences can have no autonomous space outside the discourse of natural sciences.

The larger scenario in the practice of social-scientific research may be characterized as that of *moderate scientism*. In this view, although social phenomena are not reduced to natural phenomena, they rather regarded, at least partially, as social constructions of human beings. However, since socially constructed phenomena have their own life, apart from the lives of individual social actors, and thus have the status of external facts of an independent social world, social reality can rightly be investigated in a scientific manner to provide explanation and predictive control. Such an investigation, among other things, will attempt to account for social events by reference to other social events, analogous to the way the natural scientist explains distinct natural events in terms of their cause-effect relationship. It is argued that social facts are explicable in terms of deterministic causal laws, and it is this belief in the causal determinism of social reality that underpins the social scientist's applying statistical methods and other scientific procedures in analysing social data.

Scientism of any sort is resisted by those who are convinced that human-social phenomena by their very nature do not admit of a natural-scientific mode of enquiry. For, they argue, social phenomena are constituted by human actions, and the notion of human action is unintelligible without reference to such cognate concepts as human agency, motives, beliefs, desires and purposes, which lend meaning and significance to human actions. And once meaningfulness becomes a regulative feature of human actions, social reality itself, in as much as it consists of human actions, becomes meaning-imbued or subjectively significant. Once the domain of human sciences comes to comprise meaning and purpose, the appropriate mode of this enquiry can only consist in reason-giving explanation – an explanation of social phenomena in terms of the reasons of participant human agents for bringing about the phenomena in question. Human sciences therefore constitute a *sui generis* discourse characterized by rational intelligibility (that is, teleological explanation) rather than causal-nomological generalization.

For some thinkers, the reason/cause distinction sharply demarcates the boundary between the human sciences and the natural sciences in terms of the dichotomy of *understanding* and *explanation*. It is alleged that whereas the natural scientist seeks to explain natural phenomena by subsuming particular events under general laws, the practitioner of the human sciences should seek to understand the phenomena of the human world as objectifications of the human mind. And understanding phenomena as expressions of mind is not like explaining them as the effect of causes, and the human world is not to be understood as a deterministic causal order of necessary uniformities just as natural science has formulated to describe the physical world. The human sciences are *historical*, which means that although it is possible to discover regularities that have held in the past, their validity is historically limited: they can never bind or determine what may appear in the future.

The above is a *hermeneutic* view on the nature of human sciences – a view that emphasizes the interpretative nature of social understanding by way of according centrality to the intentional or signifying character of the human agent. Since the knowledge sought here is of the *human* world, the life-world of our 'lived-experience', to which we are related in a different way from our relation to the non-human world of physical phenomena, this knowledge cannot but be achieved through an interpretative understanding of the human subjective point of view of the agents concerned.

If the 'meaningfulness' of social existence makes the human sciences hermeneutic or a matter of interpretative understanding, then the language of the human sciences can never be detached or neutral in the way the language of the natural sciences is. This is because the explanatory concepts that figure in the language of the human sciences are embedded in, and partially defined by, the social practices which constitute the object of social explanation. For example, if the technical concept of 'liquidity preference' that figures in the language of economics is to have its explanatory value at all, it must be logically tied to actual or practical concepts like money, profit and risk – that is concepts which are embedded in, and meaningful in the web of, the social practice of economic transaction. It seems therefore that the concepts of social explanation are given to the practitioner of social sciences in advance by the form of social life under investigation; and the meaning of these concepts derives from the part they play in the practice of particular social forms of life.

Given the hermeneutical character of the social or human sciences, and the fact that the meaning of social concepts is inextricably bound up with specific social practices which may vary from society to society, it looks as though there can be no spatio-temporally invariant objective matter of the social fact. Historical context-relativity of the meaningfulness of social practices would thus rule out, or at least cast suspicion upon, the possibility or admissibility of cross-cultural concepts and thereby undercut the generalizing effort to find sociological uniformities across cultures. Cultural relativism may therefore prove to be a decisive refutation of the alleged objectivity of the social sciences as well as its alleged scientism.

A more radical corollary of the above line of thinking is that the question of both objectivity and rationality in social sciences loses its ground altogether. That is to say, the rationality or irrationality of a social practice cannot be determined by reference to objectively available criteria – criteria drawn from outside the practice concerned. Criteria of rationality are, it may be held, *internal* to the practice in the sense that the given practice is rational if it is meaningful to the participants of the practice. And the social concepts or beliefs underlying the practices in questions acquire their meaning from the part they play in the relevant social practices.

If cultural relativism is right, it would not only exorcise the ghost of scientism in the human sciences, but also threaten them with the risk of total loss of objectivity. Yet, from within the hermeneutic quarter the voice of objectivity has been forcefully raised in the universalizing slogan of 'fusion of horizons'. The idea is that although there is no objective, prejudice-free, presuppositionless method of discovering the social fact of the matter, and that there is no transcendental entry-point for any enquiry into social reality which is not paved by the sediments of the historically given socio-cultural environment of the enquirer, there still is the possibility of a conversation of mankind in some universal terms, perhaps through progressive diminution of the most local predilections of the enquirers. Is this really possible? Can objectivity be retrieved through such a dialogical mode of hermeneutic enquiry?

A reflective overview of the foregoing account of the nature of human sciences will confirm the point that the ideas of objectivity, truth and rationality are drawn from their paradigmatic uses in the discourse of natural science. These key ideas are believed to be all characterized by intellectual detachment or cognitive transparency – indeed the most important necessary feature of epistemological adequacy. But it may be questioned whether any enterprise of human knowledge is in fact such a dispassionate pursuit of mirroring objective reality or truth; whether, that is, any human epistemic search is truly free from specific human interests altogether. Indeed, not only has this question been raised, but it has also been claimed that, far from being a mirroring of reality, human knowledge (or science) is always constituted by specific interests, which in turn guide the selection of 'truths' and govern the form in which they are presented as knowledge. Thus the very idea of knowledge becomes unrecognizably saturated with interest-relative ideology. And the dominant ideology assumes the role of power to legitimize the knowledge concerned. The big question here is whether the so-called notion of detached objective knowledge is after all a masquerade of the *politics* of knowledge.

The argument of interest-relativity is not the only challenge levelled against objective knowledge. Epistemological skepticism about foundationalism – the claim that knowledge is objectively valid when it is founded upon beliefs or statements that are absolutely certain – has shaken our cherished ideals of objectivity. Boundaries of discourses, such as the demarcation line drawn between natural-science discourse and human-science discourse, have been held to be unjustified. The privilege attached to transparent scientific discourse has been relegated to what is often described as the "mythology of logocentrism" – that is, words or signs are essentially signified by something that endows them with identity and constancy of meaning. Instead, opacity or indeterminacy of meaning and endless play of differences (as opposed to sameness) are said to shape language.

This post-modern outlook is explicitly iconoclastic in as much as it reveals, by its deconstructive irradiation, the mythical bedrock of discourse or language which sustains the theoretically pregnant epistemic notions like objectivity and truth. It thus puts into doubt the epistemological credibility not just of the human sciences, but also that of the so-called 'hard' sciences. The question pertinent here is whether radical skepticism is inevitable, or the alleged iconoclasm misconceived.

The essays, in this collection, that concern themselves with the issue of objectivity in human or social sciences, do not take each of the above-mentioned problems. But the essays together touch upon all such problems somehow or other, and some deal the objectivity issue with particular attention.

The opening essay, by Rajeev Bhargava, discusses the fundamental question of what makes something *social*, a question that must be answered in more or less clear terms in order that one gets a fairly good grip upon the nature of social enquiry. Bhargava gives an answer in a manner that imaginatively defends Durkheim's view that "the social consists of the form of acts and representations, both individually and collectively realized, that are external and resistant to biological individuals on whom they supervene." Durkheim is famous for advocating the objectivity of social facts, and the autonomy of social explanation based on a *sui generis* social reality. The two crucial features of a social fact are, as stated above, *externality* and *resistance*.

The externality of social facts is their existence outside any individual consciousness. Being outside of us, social facts are endured by us. And the fact that we have to endure social facts signifies the feature of resistance. Social facts put resistance on us in the sense that they are like moulds into which we are forced to cast our actions and representations. Although we are not imprisoned in our social world, we cannot break lose from it entirely without struggle, largely because social facts offer resistance to us.

Mohini Mullick encounters the problem of objectivity as the problem of the scientific nature of the knowledge of society. She traces the systematic ambition of scientific objectivity in social knowledge to Auguste Comte's positivism, and then traverses a path of conceptual survey through Durkheim to Max Weber and Karl Marx. What is focused by the first part of Mullick's essay is the very interesting way the problem of objectivity figures in a Marxist conception of social reality. The scientific approach of social enquiry for Marx is not so much aimed at validity as at the discernment and exposition of contradictions in social process. It is not "true objectivity predicated on consensus and social solidarity," but "false objectivities, the reifications born of the conflict of mutually inconsistent symbolic universes," that have to be demonstrated by critical social enquiry. Thus, for Marx, an objective social analysis and explanation means an examination of social relations; for it is social relations that underpin the true character of social reality.

In the second part of her essay, Mullick shifts the ball of objectivity from the court of social sciences to that of natural sciences, and discusses how, during the second half of the twentieth century, there has appeared a powerful critique of the notion of objectivity in the philosophical discourse on natural sciences. She charts the map of that critique right from Karl Popper's criticism of Radical Empiricist philosophy of science to Thomas Kuhn's attack on the alleged rationality of objective science, and finally to the radical sociology of science, the so-called Strong Programme of Barnes and Bloor, that argues that social factors operate indiscriminately in all knowledge situations. The essence of all such critiques is that any two different belief systems have different ways of synthesizing information and processing experience, which means that we can speak of different *kinds* of objectivity. And science itself may be seen as a belief system, subscribing to its own changing set of objective truths.

Mullick concludes, with an air of irony and *à la* Kuhn, that if theory choice is made on the basis of a curious mixture of objective situation and subjective preferences even in the natural sciences, how much more is the weight of objectivity at stake in the social sciences is well conceivable. Mullick leaves us wondering whether we have come to a full circle: "The social sciences sought their paradigm in the methods of the natural sciences. Their objectivity was to be scientific objectivity. At the end of the day we are confronted with the strong argument that scientific objectivity is in fact social. So where do we go from here?"

The rise and preponderance of the hermeneutical approach to the study of social reality is also a reflection on the inadequacy or inappropriateness of the natural-scientific paradigm of objective enquiry into human phenomena. Rajan Gurukkal, in his essay "History, Hermeneutics and Methodological Objectivity", contrasts what he calls the "hermeneutically secured objectivity" with the so-called scientific history. Objectivity, as far as history is concerned, lies in the "methods of self-scrutiny and in the confessions of historians" that enable appropriate hermeneutic evaluation. It is not so much the possibility of empirically verifiable primary experience that constitutes the criterion of historical knowledge; it is rather in the understanding of the conditions that make such historical knowledge possible that captures the objectivity of historical knowledge. Methodological self-reflexivity geared to checking the veracity of the historian's ideas is thus meant to signify the objectivity of historical understanding.

Gurukkal draws our attention to the contemporary interdisciplinary social science methodology comprising an extensive collection of conceptual tools and frameworks of comprehension such as Marxism, Critical Theory, Functionalism, Structuralism, Structuralist Marxism, Phenomenology, Substantivism, Semiology, Deconstruction, Discourse analysis, Narratology, Feminism and Post-Modernism. His point is that a comprehensive study of hermeneutic historical methodology draws upon lessons from all these meta-narratives and conceptual formulations.

Remarking on the method of discourse analysis as proposed by Foucault, Gurukkal says that Foucault's discursive history unravels peoples' self-images that are actually, but unknowingly, formed in the light of what others construe us as. Discursive history thus attains hermeneutically secured objectivity through self-reflexivity and self-criticism. But, despite all methodological advantages of discourse analysis in nuancing subtle social phenomena, Gurukkal speaks in defense of the superiority of Marxism as a social theory: "Historical Materialism remains the only paradigm to theorize the present as descent from structures of the past, as a rigorous theory of the distinctive dynamics of social development as a whole."

In "Postmodernism and Social Sciences," Gurpreet Mahajan critically examines the post-modern theoretical perspective and its implications for the study of social sciences. Mahajan conceptualizes her essay into two halves – one, the negative agenda and the other, the affirmative agenda of postmodernism. In its negative theoretical stance, postmodernism is anti-foundationalist, anti-essentialist, and clearly opposed to the Enlightenment search for invariable laws of history. All meta-narratives are rejected as false paradigms of human historicality, insofar as they focus on social structure and presumed laws of historical development by neglecting the role of agency and consciousness, and thereby obscuring the particular in history. Surely, nothing can be more damaging to the objective aspirations of rationalist universalism that underlie the explanatory programmes of a grand narrative of human history.

In the affirmative agenda, Mahajan highlights, on the one hand a kind of epistemological open-endedness, which is paralleled, on the other hand, by open-ended and plural historical processes. All truth claims, even those embodied in scientific theories, provide plural, diverse and heterogeneous descriptions of the world. Likewise, human history embodies diverse projects that human beings have embarked on at different moments in time and space, thereby presenting societies or communities of diverse styles and outlooks.

What is of interest in Mahajan's discussion of the implications of postmodernism for social sciences is the picture of symmetry between the *epistemological* and the *existential,* such that the existential is mapped on to the epistemological and *vice versa.* If knowledge or truth – claims are not bound within any theoretical closure, and multivocality or plurality of meaning is the hallmark of all texts, then freedom becomes a core existential norm, which amounts to legitimizing the emergence of new social movements. The same existential norm lends philosophical support to the various contemporary social struggles such as of women, gays, greens, blacks, indigenous people and marginalized population. The postmodernist defense of plurality voices the concerns and the reality of multi-cultural societies.

Towards the end of her essay, Mahajan draws our attention to certain counterintuitive consequences of the postmodern theoretical perspective on social analysis. The defense of indeterminacy and incoherence would make schizophrenia the norm of everyday life. And the denial of narrative continuity and understanding would jeopardize both social life and social interaction. Likewise, the postmodern celebration of multivocality and plurality of meaning would tend to generate norms that vitiate social existence, communication, understanding and explanation. The absence of any discussion of structural constraints would reduce contingency to the play of chance. Most of all, rejection of fixity of meaning would rule out commitment to political struggles, which seek to fix meaning.

In "The Limitations of the Objectivity Paradigm" TVS Ramamohan Rao has argued for a "flexible interpretation of objectivity" in view of the difficulty in generating a single objective explanation of phenomena, like human behavior, where individual differences are more pressing than commonalities. Rao reinforces his own point by alluding to Feyeraband's radical claim that, in such cases, acknowledging the differences is the essence of objectivity even if it means lack of explanation.

One thought-provoking claim that Rao makes is that it does not seem possible to construct a logical formalism to identify so-called objective facts, whether in natural or in social sciences. The identification and specification of facts will remain more or less culture-bound and time-oriented.

Talking about theoretical constructs in science, Rao contends that there is no such thing as an objective method of choosing such constructs for explanatory purposes. The choice of a certain construct can be said to be subjective even in physical sciences as well as mathematics. An example cited to this effect is the quantum theory in contrast to the wave theory.

Limiting the scope of objectivity to logical consistency of scientific theory, Rao rules out the possibility of objectively deciding between competing theories. Between theories incommensurable with one another but equally consistently explanatory of the phenomenon in question, *logical consistency* alone is really *the* correct one. An example referred to from the social sciences is that of Keynesian macroeconomic theory concerning national income. The theory is objective only to the extent that it fits into a logically consistent system. It lacks objectivity in the sense that it is not the *only* logically consistent approach to the explanation of national income. For, as Rao cites, there are at least two other logically consistent approaches to the same phenomenon, namely the classical theory and the rational expectations approach.

In view of the above limitations, Rao concludes with the suggestion that the minimal standards of objectivity should consist in (a) stating the assumptions of facts being used as premises, (b) laying down the logical method of deduction, and (c) drawing all the conclusions in a verifiable form (from the logical viewpoint).

That human social reality is collectively constituted by human agents, that it is the self-creation of human kind, is taken by Bijoy Boruah as a distinctive feature that differentiates the object of social-scientific enquiry from that of natural-scientific enquiry. Boruah's essay, "Social Reality and Social Theory", presses the point that any social phenomena are what they essentially are because human agents view these phenomena as *expressions* of their own desires and aspirations, motives, intentions, and actions. One important consequence of the subjective constitution of social reality is therefore held to be the inadequacy, and often inappropriateness, of causal explanation of social phenomena. Nomological causal explanation is appropriate only when the explanandum is conceivable in ahistorical terms. Natural phenomena, which are explained in law-governed causal terms, are such that their past history is scarcely relevant to an explanation of their present behavior.

By contrast, when we are concerned with an understanding of human beings and their actions, their past history is very much part of the present situation. Human beings and their social circumstances are all essentially historical, and this historicality renders the character of human reality *opaque* to the explanatory method of nomological objectivity. Historical contingency poses a permanent problem in the way of typifying human beings and their actions for the purpose of subsuming them under socio-psychological laws. It also poses the further problem of prediction of human actions on the basis of any regularity noticed in their past. As a prominent example of this uncertainty of social theory, Boruah cites the case of the breakdown of the Soviet Union and the eventual fall of the Berlin wall.

In the second part of his essay, Boruah highlights a significant disanalogy between social theory and physical theory. The disanalogy concerns the way theory (or knowledge) relates to practice in the two domains of discourse, social and natural. A natural-scientific theory relates to practice in an obvious way, and the relation is external. For instance, the application of the knowledge of transfer of kinetic energy results in transformation of earlier inconvenient practice of dealing with heat in actual human living condition. But the practice it transforms is not what the theory is about. One can accept the theory and yet the practice can remain unchanged, provided one does not wish or decide to put the theory into practice.

In contrast, social theories are intrinsically about practices in that a society is, among other things, a set of institutions and practices. Acceptance of the theory would result in transforming the practice to the extent that the theory transforms the self-understandings of the participants of the practice. A social theory is nothing but a theoretical formulation and articulation of a social practice and its norms, aiming at replacing or extending society's pre-theoretical understanding of the practice. Hence, the practice is internally related to the theory.

In her second essay "An Ethno-Social Science for India: Towards Objectivity in Understanding?", Gurpreet Mahajan introduces ethno-social science as a self-conscious attempt facing the predicament of the fact/value distinction in social sciences. The predicament is how an objective understanding of social reality be possible given the acknowledged presence of values in the social domain. The ethno-social scientist's holds that objectivity is jeopardized only when one imposes culturally alien views, or norms incommensurate with the social domain of study. In other words, objectivity is assured provided we study the object through its own native conceptual structure.

Mahajan is a sharp critic of McKim Marriott's attempt of constructing an ethno-methodology for the study of the Indian social reality. Making a plea for an Indian ethno-social science that constructs its hermeneutic scheme with the "natural categories" of Indian social and cultural reality – categories inherent in Indian self-representation – Marriott wishes to take a cultural leap so as to become the "other", to be the "authentic" Indian cultural voice. But Mahajan detects a glaring inconsistency at the heart of this programme. While Marriott emphasizes the need of recovering the "civilization's own categories", he, on the other hand, suggests also that we need to build a *general* model of the culture under study. Further, Mahajan alleges that while constructing an Indian ethno-social science, Marriott goes beyond culture's own representation and draws upon resources available to him from Western anthropological thought. This speaks loudly of how our ways of thinking are ineradicably shaped by our historical consciousness.

Mahajan's criticism of Marriott's programme points towards its failure in recognizing the "historicity of the other" that it sets out to understand. What emerges as a result is an ahistorical and essentialist picture of Indian culture. Indeed, the turn towards dehistoricization is already implicit in the act of searching for an essentialist form. And in taking the categories embodied in ancient Hindu texts as the defining features of the Hindu/Indian universe, including the present cultural state of affairs of the land, the civilizational picture of India is projected as essentially unchanging or static. This is no understanding of the "other", but a misunderstanding, because any understanding is essentially trying to make sense of a text – a culture, civilization or practice – historically. Marriott's ethno-sociological construct belies social understanding precisely because the construct purporting to understand the other in its self-representational image does not accord with the principle of historicity.

Part II
Culture and Tradition

Granted that there is the existential order of human reality as the object of the human sciences, and the intentional order of meaning, value and purpose all sustained by a reflexive consciousness unique to the cultural character of the human race, any mature understanding of the nature of human reality will be bound up with the question of the cultural historical heritage as constituting the civilizational matrix of human existence. It is the civilizational matrix of human history and culture that is known as *tradition.* Inasmuch as the human situation is essentially historical, its self-conscious cultural manifestations continually, although unconsciously, draw upon a symbolically sedimented past that remains mysteriously alive in the memory of the collective psyche. The past, pregnant with a rich plethora of hermeneutic content, animates the cultural life of the present, and thereby shapes the order and style of life in culture-specific ways.

Tradition, in the sense explicated above, is a foremost topic of the human studies in general. Though the various human sciences do not address themselves directly to an elucidation of the concept of tradition as it figures in the cultural map of humanity, these sciences tacitly presuppose the role of tradition in shaping the character of social practices and institutions. In a way, the centrality of the role of tradition can hardly be bypassed in ascertaining the issue of objectivity in systematic human inquiries as the social sciences are.

The historical constitution of social reality ineluctably places social beings in a cultural space that has a *horizontal* background. Tradition is that horizontal background, and it is clear that the cultural image of society embodies a symbolic significance that cannot fully be deciphered without properly making sense of the background. And if socio-cultural diversity and specificity be anthropological facts inviting social-scientific study, then to ignore the peculiarly local features of a cultural practice with its unique hermeneutic roots in particular traditions could be a case myopia. This may even have the far reaching implication that there is no monolithic, trans-cultural objective conceptual paradigm to constitute a non-relative mode of social explanation.

The relation between a specific form of social life and the background tradition that needs to be alluded to in accounting for that specificity of life-form, therefore, has a decisive consequence for the assessment of the feature of objectivity in the human sciences. For the possibility of cultural relativism and social localism may considerably limit the scope of objective explanatory criteria. But more importantly, the determination of the enduring outlook of a cultural form of life by its intrinsic moorings in the background tradition would render the problem of understanding social reality unavoidably tradition-specific. There may be a reasonable skepticism about the availability of a neutral set of rationalist concepts and categories to be unquestioningly deployed in social enquiry as such. On the contrary, it may be more reasonable, and even necessary, to develop concepts and categories of social enquiry by being sensitive to the depth of a society's cultural heritage or enduring history.

The attuning of social-scientific conceptual vocabulary or hermeneutic repertoire to tradition-specific *Weltanschauung* would of course be incumbent on a social theorist in order that there be no disconcerting mis-match between conceptual apparatus and social reality. If this is an insight of what is true of social reality, then it presupposes that the cultural efflorescence of human consciousness is perhaps determined by historical contingencies through and through, and the diversity of traditions in human history is a consequence of that determination. In that case, the rationalist programme of a universalist paradigm of social enquiry modelled on the nomological paradigm of natural science would betray a deep truth about human history and social reality.

On these considerations there may be debates, but such debates would bring to the fore the question of understanding traditions. The idea of a tradition is the idea of ourselves as we emerge with our cultural peculiarities. We have no other route to take than trace our journey back to our enduring cultural ancestry, if we are to understand ourselves or our specific identity in the human world. It therefore looks quite right that the general issue of the human sciences be meaningfully related to the shaping of social reality by the tradition that forms its inarticulate background.

Such issues about what it is to make sense of the idea of a tradition, and the crucial base this idea forms in theorizing about social reality, demand much larger space of discussion than what is given in this book. There are only three essays in this book that address themselves directly to the question of tradition, and they all take up the question with special reference to understanding the *Indian* tradition. This choice of concentrating on the Indian tradition is understandable in that the authors of each of these three essays draw their deep intellectual and cultural nourishment from their indigenous environment and history. One question that arises in this very context is whether the core spirit of a particular tradition is intrinsically such that only those who are "spiritually" internal to the tradition can truly illuminate and articulate the seemingly inscrutable core. An "externalist" excursus into a particular tradition might be missing the sight of the deeper and more enduring inner recesses of a cultural heritage.

That an externalist view on a particular tradition is far from being undistorted or sacrosanct is already reflected in the well-known criticisms of Orientalism, the so-called Indological theory of the Indian tradition developed by the Western colonial intellectuals. Orientalism as an intellectual movement shot into prominence in the wake of the colonial domination of India. In "Tradition as Narrative" Rajan Gurukkal ironically says that the mode of perception of the traditionality of the Indian way of life is entirely non-traditional and non-Indian: "What was perceived as tradition was actually modernity, and what the act [of Orientalist textualization] replicated as tradition was the Western perception of Indian past."

Gurukkal's essay is mainly concerned with highlighting the narrative character of a tradition, both textualized and pre-textualized narrative. While the so-called Indian tradition is textualized largely by the Western Orientalists, and the traditionality manifest in this textual objectification is coeval with colonial modernity, there is also a pre-modern or traditional consciousness of tradition as an unwritten narrative writ large on the practical consciousness of the indigenous people. This is the distinction between consciousness of tradition *as peoples' self-image* and tradition *as peoples' lived reality*. While the former is the self-articulated version of the latter, the latter is "natural, transcendental, and hardly amenable to textualization" and also "the absent cause" of the former.

Gurukkal's other major point is his emphatic characterization of the Indian tradition as "a historiographic construct and not historical". One central objectification of such a historiographic construct is the grand narrative of Hinduism, according to which the Indian tradition is essentially Hindu tradition. In Gurukkal's opinion this is erroneous, and "a structured outcome of colonial misrepresentation of the plurality and diversity of countless micro-traditions that weave the fabric of the Indian people." The historical truth is that multiple micro-traditions co-existed, interacted and influenced one another, through discontinuity and process of reconstitution. It would therefore be a betrayal of truth, and a travesty of history, to try to inscribe a single macro-tradition on the multitudinous surface of Indian culture, howsoever meticulous the search for a common core may be.

While Gurukkal's voice has the clear non-essentializing tone that resounds with the assertion of cultural pluralism, G.C. Pande is quite intent on essentializing Indian culture in terms of its unity in diversity. In "Understanding Indian Culture: The Question of its Unity and Diversity", Pande considers the strong hold of Indian culture to be the idea of *Sanatana dharma* – the idea of *dharma* as timeless vision that encapsulates spiritual tolerance of diverse ways of life. The catholicity of the Indian mind is best expressed in the cryptic but highly charged formula, "live and let live". Pande would perhaps say, in response to the anti-essentialist outlook of Gurukkal, that it is this normative principle of *Sanatana dharma*, deeply entrenched in the cultural psyche of India, that accounts for the possibility of the co-existence of a multitude of micro-traditions in India.

Presumably, what explains the catholicity and unifying force of the *Sanatana dharma* of the Indian tradition is the belief in spiritual equality. This transcendental belief, born out of the metaphysical philosophies of the Indian "darsanic" tradition, must be the source of the innermost aspirations of Indian culture that Pande alludes to in his essay.

A debate can be conceived of as taking place over the question of whether tradition or culture is to be understood in terms of the actual manifest material processes of human history, or it should be judged by reference to a certain transcendental core that may not always reflect on the surface of social history. Judging from the thrust of Gurukkal's essay one would think that he subscribes to the former view. Pande, on the other hand, would seem to subscribe to the latter view. He advances a cautionary note against the tendency to equate the defining characteristics of a culture or tradition with its material or other expressive features. For that equation is likely to overlook the more enduring and underlying features that embody a culture's deeper self-consciousness and innermost human aspirations.

While it is quite usual to talk about tradition *vis-à-vis* modernity, A.K. Saran is vehemently opposed to such a pairing or conceptual juxtaposition. In his most challenging essay "On Tradition," Saran contends that the very pairing of modernity and tradition commits what he calls "the fallacy of anachronism". So much so that the concept of tradition "is not explicable in terms of distinction or contradistinction from any other concept or family of concepts." Especially, modernity cannot be historically linked with tradition because the ontological planes of the two are entirely incommensurate with one another. Whereas modernity is a temporal phenomenon manifesting itself in the contingent order of history, tradition is timeless, formless, transcendental, suprapersonal and non-manifest.

Saran's transcendentalization of the concept of tradition is a clear reflection of his wholehearted allegiance to classical Indian Upanisadic metaphysics. It is understandable that anyone who grounds tradition in transcendental metaphysics would disclaim, as Saran does, that tradition is a "humanistic" or "sociological" category. It is rather held to be "a sort of anthropo-metaphysical idea", which is the complex idea of the relation of human beings to "the eternal centre, the void, the *Parabrahma*". Admitting this relation to be a mystery, Saran writes: "It [i.e. tradition] is not identical with the centre, but is mysteriously related to the centre from which it flows and to which it returns." Evidently, this conception of tradition replaces the anthropocentric world view by a cosmocentric one, and posits a timeless cosmic centre by dint of which the temporal order of manifest human reality may be set in a time-transcending existential direction.

Saran's idea of tradition draws upon two specific theoretical formulations: one of Marco Pallis's four-fold definition of a traditional civilization, the other of Bhartrihari's hierarchical theory of language. In linking human spatio-temporal existence with a timeless absolute that sets the time-transcending existential direction, Saran alludes to Marco Pallis's notion of a traditional – and normal – civilization having its roots in a doctrine of the purely metaphysical order, from which all other constituents of a tradition – social, ethical, artistic down to the most ordinary practices of life – derive their sanction. Such a civilization takes tradition as its source of inspiration, of Revelation. When human life becomes a way of "verifying" the timeless metaphysical ideals and attitudes, the human subject is led to successive positions that enable him/her to actualize the truths that Revelation communicates.

What is the truth that Revelation communicates? In order that the truth of Revelation may at least be glimpsed, Saran finds it convenient to invoke Bhartrihari's theory of language. It is Saran's central claim that human consciousness is *self*-reflexive: the human subject, by the very nature of its subjectivity, is ineluctably drawn to the ontological self-interrogation, "Who am I?" The answer to this question can be made available to the subject in a graduated and successive process that is neatly mapped on to the hierarchically arranged four levels of language: *vaikhāri, madhyamā, paśyantī* and *parā*. While the *para* level of language coincides with the state of the subject as one with the primordial unity, the two levels of *vaikhāri* and *madhyamā* correspond to a "rupture of the primordial unity". The true meaning of human self-reflexivity is, for Saran, the potentiality of human consciousness to overcome this existential rupture and reintegrate itself into the primordial cosmic unity.

One might interpret Saran's theory as meaning that the availability of "normal" civilization depends upon a human social order where the human subject understands the ultimate truth to be that of cosmocentric non-dualism, even when the subject's actual living condition is apparently shaped by anthropocentric dualism of the self and the other. The so-called transcendence of the temporal through the inspiration of the timeless absolute order is an utterly recondite way of putting the simple civilizational truth that the life of the lower self needs to be overcome so that one becomes the higher self.

I

Objectivity in Social Understanding

1

What Makes Something Social?

RAJEEV BHARGAVA

Let us consider the following examples of social entities: a priest; capital; the high table; the state of being unemployed; the flag symbolizing the nation; the prime minister requesting the dissolution of the assembly; fascism. What must all these objects, persons, ideas, states of affairs, actions, and events possess in order to be classed as *social*, as distinct from merely physical or mental phenomena? What in general is it for something to be or have social as distinct from mental and material properties? Can a criterion be general enough to subsume within it a variety of phenomena, demarcating the lot at the same time from other types of entities and properties?[1]

A fairly common answer to these questions is to assert that the 'social' consists of a pattern of behavior of two or more persons involving a set of rules, norms, rewards and punishments, rights and powers and so on. Thus, Homans claims that "for a behavior to be social implies that when a person acts in a certain way he is at least rewarded or punished by the behavior of another person".[2] Skorupski argues that a social characteristic is one whose possession is constituted purely or partly in the existence of rules.[3] On Emmett's view it is the presence of norms that guarantees the existence of the social.[4] For Elster, the social entails the existence of a pattern of interdependencies between persons involving choices, rewards and preference structures.[5] Finally, Cohen argues that a description is social "if it entails an ascription to persons, specified or unspecified, rights or powers *vis-à-vis* other persons."[6] I believe these views to be seriously deficient for at least two reasons. First, they work with a view of the social that is too restrictive, leaving out entities or properties that cannot be relegated to the mental or the material world. Secondly, they pay inadequate attention to the possibility of the reduction of the social to the conjunction of the physical and the mental. If the defining characteristics of the social are nothing but physical or mental properties, then we are left without a distinctive conception of the social. The requirement, therefore, that we have a conception of the social that is general enough to pick out all social entities or properties and distinctive enough to demarcate these from all other types of entities and properties, is not met. To substantiate these points, I examine in detail the views of Cohen.

For Cohen, a person is not a priest as such nor is a piece of wood by nature a high table; they become so only when inserted into a web of social relations. And not all relations are social. For example, the interaction of two persons carrying an object together does not have a necessary social content. It does only when the action is performed in pursuit of an agreement or under the authority of someone, however. In itself, ploughing a field or making a shoe is not social, but it is so when done in exchange for a wage. Therefore, there exists distinction between the material and social description of things. For example, ploughing a field is a material description of an action because it does not entail the ascription of rights and powers *vis-à-vis* other persons, i.e., no social relations. It follows that from the material characteristics of a thing, one cannot simply deduce its social characteristics. The presence of one does not entail the existence of the other. For Cohen, it shows the irreducibility of the social to the material.

A few clarifications will be in order before we proceed any further. First, Cohen or (or Cohen's Marx) uses the term 'material' to cover both the physical and the mental.[7] Boring a hole in the ground is a material activity, but so also is the technical know-how necessary for it. Technological activity is material as is the more speculative, scientific activity. Second, by suggesting that the mere act of carrying something together (or ploughing a field) is not social, he claims that the other-regarding feature of an action is not sufficient for rendering it social; it must be other-regarding in a special way. It is not enough that action be intentionally oriented to the other. Only those other-regarding actions are social whose intentional content contains an ascription of rights and powers *vis-à-vis* other persons. To be social, then, an action must possess an intentional content that is already social. Likewise, an object, event or state of affairs is social if it possesses or entails the presence of a social intention.

Let us apply Cohen's criterion to the following sets of examples:

1. The desire to eat/desire to eat beef rather than dog-meat/the taboo on dog-meat.
2. Walking/walking upright/walking upright to defy a superior.
3. Bronze/a statue in bronze/the bronze statue as a commodity for sale in the market.
4. The sensation of something external and forceful/the idea of god/the idea of god performing a distinct ideological function.

Clearly all items placed first in each set are either physical or mental entities. Similarly, items placed last are social entities. This much would be agreed by almost anyone wishing to make a contrast between the social and the material. However, in Cohen's view, the second item in each set is material. The desire to eat beef, walking upright, the bronze statue and the idea of god involve only physical and mental characteristics and therefore are not social. They do not entail the ascription of either rights or powers *vis-à-vis* any other person. While it is true that rights or powers are not entailed by these descriptions, their inclusion in the material world rather than the social world appears odd. For we know that the desire to eat beef is not universal and particular societies have a lot to do with why it is not. We also know that the idea of statue or that of god is specific to societies and could not just have sprung arbitrarily from the minds of the individuals. Of course, to have to come into existence in one society and not in other societies, does not by itself show that the entity in question is social, but at the very least, it provides some basis, however weak, for the view that the society in question has something to do with its existence. It follows that if we wish to include them in our inventory of social entities, we must fish out some criterion that makes this possible. We must look for a criterion of the social that is general enough to include all these entities, but which continues to show these to be different from material and mental entities.

Nothing said above constitutes, even resembles an argument against Cohen's classification. But further examples help underline the oddity of his criterion: a solitary prayer; writing a diary; going alone on a summer holiday; the use of language; fashions; norms of consumption; and friendship. On Cohen's criterion, all these are material or mental or both but not social because they do not entail an ascription of rights and powers to persons. The first three, quite simply, involve no other person and therefore cannot be social; but the remaining do, but are not social because they do not entail the ascription of rights and powers. This result is counter-intuitive. Something about each of these examples inhibits us from excluding them from the social world.

Here, Cohen might reply that rights and powers need not be entailed but be simply presupposed by every particular description of entity, property or act. But I fail to see how rights and powers are presupposed by, say, the act of reading a newspaper or brushing one's teeth every morning. Yet, both these acts seem neither merely physical nor mental and seem to presuppose some fact about the particular societies where they occur. Something is amiss in Cohen's classification.

I think an analogy can help grasp what is wrong in Cohen's way of marking the distinction. Humans are biological organisms, clearly distinguished from the rest of the physical world by virtue of certain characteristics that they alone possess. Undoubtedly, their outstanding, even defining, feature is their capacity for self-consciousness. Now it would be a great mistake to take this feature as the critical one that distinguishes them from the inanimate, physical world. It would be even worse if this were believed to be the individuating feature of the biological creatures more generally. This would result in relegating almost all remaining biological entities to the inanimate world. Man is a biological entity, but from this it does not follow that any feature that is capable of distinguishing him would also distinguish all other biological entities from the rest of the physical world. The flaw in the classification of Cohen and others is analogous to the one mentioned above. A very specific form assumed by the social is picked out as the mark distinguishing the social from the material, thus relegating a large class of social entities to the material world. Since the social so commonly takes the form of persons involving rights or power, it has been confused with the idea of social in general. Although every instance rights and power is social, not everything social involves rights and powers. The criterion offered by Cohen is too narrow and restrictive to do justice to the wide variety of entities and properties that, to my mind, are social.

However, let us suppose that the criterion provided by Cohen does cover all the relevant social phenomena. One might still persist in asking: is the social irreducible to the material. As we have seen, for Cohen this is indeed the case because from a material description one cannot derive a social one. This argument is mistaken. Consider an event, say the death of a person. From the mere description of the death of the person, one cannot derive how the death occurred. A person can die in a number of ways, but from this fact it does not follow that these different ways of dying are different in kind from each other or from the event of death itself. All of these can equally be provided with a material description. Failure of logical entailment does not by itself show irreducibility. Moreover, we know that, at least on one view, logical irreducibility is compatible with nomological reducibility; indeed it is a condition of nomological reducibility. If this is so, the underivability of social from material descriptions does not show the irreducibility of one to the other.

Let us suppose, however, that neither of the considerations specified above is relevant. Does irreducibility follow on Cohen's own terms? I fear not. Recall that, for Cohen, a description is social *if* it entails the ascription of rights and powers *vis-à-vis* persons. But power can be given a wholly physical description. Even if power is taken to be an intentional notion, it remains material, for intentionality is a mental notion and, on Cohen's account, all mental properties are material. Similarly, rights are a matter of expectations and beliefs, and these are standardly taken to be mental entities. So even if it involves more than one body and mind, the social content of intentions that gives actions a social character is reducible to something physical and mental.

The mere presence of more than one body and mind might create a new property, but not a new *type* of property. A collection of material entities is still a material entity. There is nothing in Cohen's account to suggest that the social is irreducible to the material. The mere fact that entailment does not obtain, at least by itself, does not show irreducibility.

I have argued that Cohen provides a criterion, not of the social in general, but of a specific form assumed by the social. He has arbitrarily selected one particular kind of social entity and built out of it a general conception of the social, when in fact the social entity in question already presupposes another, more general, perhaps even more fundamental criterion. As a result, Cohen's concept leaves out a vast area of social life, wrongly relegating it to the physical or the mental, to what he calls the material. I have also claimed that even if this conception of the social be the most general one available, it would still fail to be an adequate concept of the *social* because it is reducible to the mental and the physical. Even if Cohen's criterion were found to have unrestricted application, covering all types of entities with something in common, it would fail to pick out anything distinctively social. Instead, it refers to a collection of mere mental and physical entities, or physical entities with physical and mental properties. I believe this to be true not only for Cohen's but also for all other criteria mentioned above. Any specification of the social in terms of rules or norms is still much too restrictive. Social entities not governed by norms or rules do exist. Moreover, rules, norms, rewards, etc., may, unless demonstrated otherwise, be reducible to physical and mental entities. We conclude then that we are as yet without a general and irreducible conception of the social.

In order to arrive at this conception, I suggest that we examine the relevant work of Durkheim. Reasons for this are fairly obvious. He was the first to seek a criterion of the social that would individuate non-material entities and properties.

Second, he tried to grapple with this problem with a methodological purpose in mind, namely, to establish the autonomy of the social sciences with respect to physics, biology and psychology. He tried to argue for autonomous social explanation on the basis of a *sui generis* social reality. This makes his work especially relevant to the philosophy of social sciences.

To begin with, let me set aside some utterly misplaced criticisms of the Durkheimian position. Durkheim has often been accused of overlooking the material substratum of the social, i.e., several biological individuals with their innate properties. This is absurd. He says, "Undoubtedly, no collective entity could be produced if there is no individual consciousness" but then goes on to add, "this is a necessary but not a sufficient condition."[8] Nor does he deny the dependence of the social phenomena upon general human nature. He says, "the general characteristics of human nature play their part in the work of elaboration from which social life results...these can be realized only if human nature is not opposed to them."[9] He even concedes that "the elementary properties from which social facts emerge are contained in the embryo within the minds of the individuals."[10] But he insists that they emerge only after "minds of the individuals have been transformed by association."[11] If social facts are to emerge, individual consciousnesses must be associated and combined in a certain way. Although human nature does not directly produce or provide a specific form to social phenomena, it certainly makes them possible. It provides the indeterminate matter that the social factors fashion and transform. Its contribution is made up of the very general states, vague and thus malleable predispositions which of themselves could not assume the definite and complex forms that characterize social phenomena, that is, if other agents did not agree to intervene. In sum, social phenomena depend on the mental and the physical, both of which make them possible, but are distinct and emergent from, and therefore, irreducible to either or both.

Putting the matter more crisply, one might say that the social is supervenient on the mental and the physical both in and outside the biological individual.

The non-individualist is also accused of failing to grant human agency its central role in social affairs. Durkheim has often been flayed, even by those sympathetic to him, for having committed this colossal blunder. But evidences from his methodological writings provide a different picture. He says: "It is true that society comprises no active forces other than those of the individuals."[12] Social things, he says, "are realized only by men, they are products of human activity."[13] I believe it to be a truism, hardly ever denied by any reasonable non-individualist, that only living, automated biological organisms of a specific type can make things move in the sense relevant here, or invest life into a non-living matter. In human societies, it is individuals who provide the 'push and pull,' the characteristics of social change and production. They constitute the primeval active elements. The social, we have already said, is supervenient on biological individuals and therefore on their activity. The social consists both of, and is dependent upon, the active biological individuals. A non-individualist contesting that the social depends on forces inherent in biological individuals does so on the pain of sheer absurdity. But he also points out that the activity of *biological* individuals is insufficient for the working of specifically *human* societies. The real matter in dispute between the individualist and the non-individualist is not whether the human agency is explanatorily crucial, but *what* kind of agency it is. For the non-individualist, the specifically human activity is not reducible to the behavior of biological individuals with their primitive or innate desires, beliefs and intentions.

So this much is clear. Social reality does not hover over and above material reality; rather it is rooted in and dependent upon it, and in particular, upon the vital movements i.e. the activity of human biological movements. This fails to specify, however, just what the social is.

It is commonly acknowledged that, for Durkheim, two characteristics distinguish the social from other phenomena: *externality* and *constraint.* Social phenomena are external to and exercise constraints over individuals. As a criterion for picking out social entities and properties, this seems highly dubious. Neither seems necessary nor sufficient for identifying the distinctively social. For a start, any natural phenomenon is both external to and exercises constraints over individuals. What then is the distinguishing mark of the social? In response, Durkheim could rightly argue that externality plus constraint are not meant to provide a definition of the social, but constitute useful guidelines for pragmatic identification during methodological research. In pragmatic contexts, one is looking for a useful and approximate guide, for only a rough specification, not for an accurate, comprehensive inventory of features by which something is sure to be identified. Sadly enough, this plea does not save the criteria, best as it is with a number of other problems.

The first centres around the constraining property of social phenomena. Clearly some social entities are both internal to individuals and do not constrain them. The ability to construct arguments belongs to individuals. *Qua* ability it does not exist outside them. Nor does it appear to constrain them in any obvious way. Of course, arguments cannot be produced independently of the rules on which they depend; but rather than constraining anyone, rules enable individuals to achieve things that cannot otherwise be realized. Individuals are able to do a large number of things by virtue of certain social characteristics and, while the exercise of the abilities may constrain other individuals, it does not in any way constrain the agent himself. Indeed, commentators have rightly noted a deep ambiguity in Durkheim's use of this notion. For him, the term "constraint" covers the authority of rules and norms, both those enabling the successful execution of actions, and those which invoke sanctions when violated, that is to say both *constitutive* and *regulative* rules; the causal influence as well as psychological compulsion of ecological factors and crowd situations; as well as the more general process of acculturation which require that individuals be trained into the ideas and values of the community.[14]

On what grounds, one might ask, do we put all these under one single rubric? Is this justifiable? More importantly, as Durkheim himself recognizes, not all of these are constraining. What then justifies the use of the word "constraint" to cover all of these phenomena? Even Durkheim's plea that his criterion suggest, not that every social fact necessarily constrains, but only that it is capable of doing so, does not validate the use of the word 'constraint' in the present context. One can put the point simply by saying, with Giddens, that social facts do not only constrain but *enable*.[15] Therefore, the use of the term "constraint", in this context, is at best misleading, However, it does not follow that some other related word cannot be used to bring together these phenomena under one rubric.

Consider now the following examples. If I follow traffic rules I shall, unless I am in Delhi, reach my workplace safely; but if I do not, I shall cause an accident, incur a fine, or at least invite abuse. If an industrialist uses modern technology and techniques of management, large profits would accrue; but if obsolete technology is employed, the industrial unit is likely to be ruined. If I speak a language shared by other members of my society, I will communicate with them; but not if I invent my own private idiolect. Traffic rules, modern technology, techniques of management, language, are social facts which exist outside any individual, have to be endured; but they enable the individual to achieve objectives at least as much as, in some other respect, they constrain. Indeed, it may be truer to say that they constrain the individual only to assist him realize his aims. But something which enables us in this way can hardly be called a constraint. If I wish to become a good painter, I must, sometime during my life, follow established masters. Is this a constraint on me, or something which would enable me to better realize my objective?

Clearly, we require a concept that subsumes properties of the social in virtue of which it is outside and endured by us, which refers to those properties of social facts which make them impervious to easy manipulation and control by individuals. Such a concept is indeed present in Durkheim's own discussion of these issues. He says: "we have seen that social facts posses this property of *resistance*. Far from being a product of our will, they determine it from without. They are like moulds into which we are forced to cast our actions. The necessity is often ineluctable. But even if we succeed in triumphing, the opposition we have encountered suffices to alert us that we are faced with something independent of ourselves."[16] Again he says: "Even when we struggle to be free from these rules and successfully break them, it is never without being forced to fight against them."[17] On Durkheim's view, we are not imprisoned in our social world. We can break lose from it but not entirely without struggle, largely because they offer resistance to us. The notion of resistance is weaker than that of constraint. To be constrained is to be virtually paralyzed, when the will of the agent is wrested away, and his freedom curtailed. On the other hand, resistance can be offered even by things which help you realize your freedom. We can therefore readily admit that all social facts are capable of offering resistance, while denying them the power to constrain. Resistance is a property possessed by those facts which constrains and those which do not. The manner in which resistance is offered differs from case to case, but the effect is much the same. Social facts deter the exercise of one's will either to enable one to achieve one's objective, or to thwart it. Though not a defining feature, the capacity to offer resistance is an essential characteristic of social phenomena.

One might now aver that for purposes of distinguishing social phenomena, the criterion of resistance is hardly better than the one involving constraint. As it is fairly obvious, natural phenomena offer resistance quite in the same sense in which social phenomena do. At this juncture it would help to underline the point behind this criterion. For Durkheim, it is meant to provide a contrast, not between physical and social, but instead between mental and social phenomena. More specifically, the intended contrast here is between individually realized mental representations and social entities. The property of resistance helps us to distinguish the social from mental representations that are internal to the individual.[18] Internally realized mental representations are within the control of the individual. On the other hand, social phenomena are outside the individual, and because they offer resistance, they are not easily manipulable. It appears then that externality and the capability of offering resistance are jointly sufficient for distinguishing the social from the mental. Social phenomena, it appears, partake of the physical and mental world, without being reducible to either or both. With physical phenomena they have in common properties that differentiate them from the mental world, and with mental phenomena they share those which distinguish them from physical entities. One implication of this is the following: Social phenomena are external to individuals and offer resistance to them, but not in the same way as do physical phenomena. Clearly, we need to dig deeper to find those phenomena that are external to individuals and offer them resistance, but are neither merely physical nor mental, though supervenient on both. What is it that is external to individual consciousness, offers resistance to individual wills, but which is constitutively different from the physical in general as well as from the biological individual with all his innate mental states?

To this question, Durkheim has two answers. As for the first, the social consists of manners of acting, thinking and feeling, and even ways of being. As to the second, it consists of collective representations and actions. Though distinct, these answers are closely related. The first answer suggests that actions and mental representations cannot exist without possessing determinate shape, a *form* which is social. Things with mental or physical components acquire social characteristics when they acquire form. But for the second answer, any collective action or representation is, by definition, social. Collective representations resemble their individual, mental counterparts, but unlike the latter, they possess features in common with the physical world: they are external to individuals who they resist. Similarly, in some respects, collective actions are like the movement of a billiard ball, but unlike them, they also possess intentionality. However, their intentional content is not wholly generated internally, by the exclusive effort of the individual. The primitive action of biological individuals may be characterized by such content, but not collective actions, whose intentional content is produced outside any given individual and has qualities of resistance. This is true not only of collective actions and representations, but also of the form of many of our individually realized actions and thoughts. If they are to resemble anything remotely human, our biological desires, perceptions and behavior are cast in social mould. Without it, our mental world is formless, our actions unstructured. This, then, is a plausible characterization of the social: It consists of the form of acts and representations, both individually and collectively realized, that are external and resistant to biological individuals on whom they supervene. This is what Durkheim means when he says that social life is neither material, nor an aggregate of individual psychological states and acts, but *sui generis*.[19]

What are the forms of representations and actions? The prime candidates for collective representations, in Durkheim's view, are concepts and categories. Together, categories form the stable grid that, by enclosing thought, render it possible. They constitute the framework of intelligence. Following Kant, Durkheim argues that categories order individual sensations into distinct experiences, but they do so in the most general way possible. Therefore, they are applicable to all types of reality. Concepts, on the other hand, have the same function as categories; but their restricted generality enables them to lend thought and experience a specificity and distinction they lack otherwise. Both are intrinsically collective and therefore distinct from any purely mental entity. What evidence or argument does Durkheim furnish for this claim? Against the empiricists and with Kant, he argues for the irreducibility of concepts to sensations. Concepts are not sensations because they are characterized by generality and necessity that correspond to nothing else in reality. Sensations and their contents, if they can be so called at all, "always rely upon a determinate object, or upon a collection of objects of the same sort and express the momentary condition of a particular consciousness; they are essentially individual and subjective. We therefore have considerable liberty in dealing with the representations of this origin."[20] On the other hand, concepts and especially categories, have a stability that sensations lack. Nor are we at liberty with respect to concepts; rather they impose themselves upon, and exercise an authority over, us. For instance, we can hardly think of an object existing outside space or time. The point can be simply put like this: sensations are the property of individuals, are momentary, unstructured and manipulable at will. If concepts and categories grew out of, or were even built out of, sensations by individuals, they would have all these characteristics. However, they posses properties that differ in kind from sensations or from any other mental entity of that sort. It follows that they are not willed and could not be subjective.

From where do they come then? Here Durkheim parts company with Kant and other apriorists for whom concepts and categories exist in the mind of individuals, and are inherent in human nature. True, for Kant, they impose themselves on us just as any other fundamental element of our nature, and are therefore objective and unmanipulable; but all the same they are mental and individual. For Durkheim this provides no explanation of concepts, however. He says: "It is no explanation of anything to say that it is inherent in human nature."[21] The correct answer for Durkheim is that these are built as a result of "an immense cooperation" of individuals, "stretches out not only in space but also in time; to make them, a multitude of mind have associated, united and combined their ideas and sentiments; a special intellectual activity is therefore concentrated in them which is infinitely richer and more complex than that of the individual."[22] Concepts then do not spring from a divine source or from the minds of individuals, but are a result of the cooperative effort of individuals. They exist outside individual minds. We receive them and therefore cannot on our own beget them. They force themselves on us, resist us and are therefore not easily manipulable. Concepts have all features of a social entity. A similar case can also be made for collective actions.

Let me now recapitulate this Durkheimian view. Sensations are private and individual. Collectively held and generated categories and concepts give these sensations a shape. It is these *informed* sensations that are experienced by human beings. Individualized experience, then, is already mediated by a social entity. Of course, being individualized, it has a distinct internal coloration, but it also possesses a communicable common meaning. Similarly, mere biological behavior is internally caused and individual in character. But no human behavior is entirely unstructured. It has a determinate shape, a form, and belongs to a type. This format or structure too is collectively generated. Individually realized action, therefore, is already, in a significant sense, social. Since no action is free of conceptual content, and content is intrinsically social, Examination of the content of individual actions will reveal their intrinsic sociality. Furthermore, when a socially mediated experience is realized not in one individual but among several individuals, we have a collective experience which is social in a robust sense. Likewise, when a socially mediated an action is realized not individually but among several individuals, we have a form of collective action which has a "thick" social character.

Let us return to some of the examples mentioned at the beginning of this paper. On Cohen's criteria, the desire to eat beef, walking upright, the bronze statue, the idea of god are material entities. On Durkheim's criteria, because they involve concepts, these are material but social entities. Individuals on their own could never develop the idea of god, an abhorrence for beef, or even imagine sculpting. All these presuppose a system of classification, conceptual scheme, a collectively produced culture sustained by humans. This suggests that two types of social facts exist: *conceptual*, or perhaps *cultural*, and *institutional*. Conceptual facts only obliquely involve social relations, while institutional facts implicate them more directly. The two are also distinguished by the fact that one of them does, but the other does not, entail the presence of some system of rights and powers. Cohen's view of the social is founded wholly on these institutional entities and fails to take into account conceptual entities. That is why it is narrow and excludes a very large number of entities, properties, states and events from the social world. Now, institutional facts also presuppose or directly involve cultural facts. This means that an institutional entity comes into being when something is inserted into an already existing social context. In other words, an institutional fact is doubly social. This precisely is what makes it strongly or maximally social. But both types of facts are social because they are produced collectively by humans. I think one of the functions of the concept of the social is to pick out entities that are collectively produced from among those which are merely given to us (within or outside us). This particular point about the social is well captured in Durkheim's account.

I believe the this Durkheimian account is along the right lines though inadequate, because the representation component in the idea of collective representation, and the collective component in the concept of collective action, are notionally misleading. I think the point may be better conveyed by using the concepts of shared meanings and practices. However, these have been the topic of another, longer paper.[23]

Notes

1. By "criterion" I mean not necessary and sufficient conditions, not a definition but merely a defensible set of conditions which an entity or a property must possess before it can be called social. Secondly, this might be taken to be an ontology of the social as well. In other words, without specifying what this relationship between the word "social" and the world is, I assume that specifying the concept is also characterizing the entity to which the word is constitutively related. I do not, therefore, see any difference, for present purposes, between elucidating the meaning of the word "social" and disclosing features of a social entity or property.
2. George C. Homans, *Social Behavior*. London: Routledge & Kegan Paul, 1961, p. 2.
3. J. Skorupski. *Symbol and Theory*. Cambridge: Cambridge University Press, 1983, p. 96.
4. D. Emmett. *Rules, Roles and Relations*. London: Macmillan, 1966.
5. Elster's views can be found in J. Elster's "Further Thoughts on Marxism, Functionalism and Game Theory," in J. Roemer (ed.),

Analytical Marxism. Cambridge: Cambridge University Press, 1986, pp. 202-220. Also in J. Elster, *Explaining Technical Change*. Cambridge: Cambridge University Press, 1979, p. 77.

6. G. A. Cohen. *Karl Marx's Theory of History*. Oxford: Oxford University Press, 1979, p. 94.
7. ibid., p. 47.
8. E. Durkheim. *The Rules of Sociological Method*. Edited by Steven Lukes; trans. W. D. Halls. Basingstoke: Macmillan, 1982, p. 129.
9. ibid., pp. 130-31.
10. ibid., p. 252.
11. ibid.
12. ibid., p. 251.
13. ibid., p. 62.
14. See Lukes, Durkheim, p. 12.
15. A. Giddens. *The Constitution and Society*. Cambridge: Polity Press, 1984, Ch. 1.
16. E. Durkheim, *op cit.*, p. 70.
17. ibid., p. 51.
18. ibid., p. 71.
19. ibid., p. 250.
20. E. Durkheim. *The Elementary Forms of Religious Life*. London: Allen & Unwin, 1976, p. 14.
21. ibid.
22. ibid., p. 16.
23. These issues are discussed at length in Rajeev Bhargava's *Individualism in Social Science*. Oxford: Clarendon Press, 1992.

2

Why Objectivity?

MOHINI MULLICK

Part I

"Why Objectivity?" may strike some as a strange question. For what could be a less controversial or more objective notion than 'objectivity'! The reason I raise it is to draw your attention, at the very outset, to the possibility that more than one sort of question regarding objectivity in the social sciences can meaningfully be posed. The sort that is uppermost in most minds, and perhaps in the minds of all practicing social scientists, would be: How do we ensure objectivity in method and, thus, in result? What are its conditions and criteria? And the like. But the philosopher's questions are often more involved, not to say, radical. And they often take the form: Why? And even, whence objectivity? They may even take the form: What is the history and what are the presuppositions underlying an intellectual tradition that so prizes objective knowledge?

One very broad answer, which perhaps needs more discussion than I can give here, is that it would be a tradition that accepts a sharp dichotomy between subject and object. I point this out because I'd like to create a mindset in which we seriously consider the fact that there could be other traditions in which the knower is not counterposed to the known, and 'knowing' itself is not thought of as a two-place predicate relating some knower *a* to some proposition *p*. Knowledge in such a tradition may be thought of as hierarchical in structure, or evolving with the individual's development, as consisting of levels or layers. It might sound trite to invoke the hackneyed contrast of knowledge as *information* and knowledge as *wisdom* – but even the triteness has some relevance here. Be that as it may, we are examining the notion of objectivity in the social sciences. And it is well to remind ourselves that these sciences did develop within the folds of western intellectual history. Thus, almost all our discussions will fall squarely within that broad tradition that, as we all recognize, contains sub-traditions, each with a different perspective, projecting divergent formulations of the problem and its solution. This is as it should be.

The task assigned to me is to provide some account of the backdrop against which the concept of objectivity has developed and been debated in the context of the understanding of social reality. So without making any contentious claims about going back to the origins of the notion – we all know what a fractious problem that is – I will still make some attempt to trace the course of the doctrine that social scientific knowledge must be objective if it is to count as *knowledge* – and even more to the point, if it is to count as *science*. The limited assumption with which we start is that the problem of objectivity is the problem of the scientific nature of the knowledge of society.

Now we could go as far back as Descartes' "clear and distinct ideas", or even to Bacon's stern warnings against the "Idols of the Mind", and no doubt even further back into western history in our search for the beginnings of the objectivistic self-understanding of the sciences. But of science in general we will talk later. For the present we go no further back than the 19th century, to the advent of Positivism, the theory of science proposed by Auguste Comte. Comte's theory can be seen as a watershed in western self-understanding. Habermas writes, in the opening sentence of his essay on Comte: "Positivism marks the end of the theory of knowledge. In its place emerges the philosophy of science".[1] This remark is significant, for it points to that moment of the history of western thought at which, and may I add, since which, human knowledge has been identified with scientific knowledge, and the knowledge of man with the scientific exploration of human and social phenomena. Comte's overriding obsessions were with order and progress. (Little wonder that then Marx called him an ass!) But order and progress must be predicated on the objective knowledge of the ordering *principles* and the *mechanisms* of progress.

Since the paradigm of objectivity is of course science itself, then sociology was to be the science by man, of man and for all men to come. This implied that all social phenomena must be amenable to explanation by laws in the manner of the natural sciences. Indeed, the organic and rational society of the future must be based on science in two ways: one, the principles of social organization will be scientific, and two, its members will adopt scientific modes of thinking now made available to mankind in the Positive stage of human intellectual evolution. Comte's conception of science has been described as phenomenalist, but it was by no means subjectivist or reductionist. For him, the human brain should be a faithful mirror of the objective order; and knowledge of this order must serve as the mind's own ordering principle. Intelligence must at all times be subordinated to fact (thus obviating the possibility of speculative metaphysics). A significant statement made by Comte in this context is that there will be "invariable natural laws that will limit in each epoch, without the possibility of serious doubt, the extent and character of political action".[2] For social facts are absolute, autonomous and completely objective.

It is clear, then, that the modern notion of social objectivity was born and developed in response to the specific historical circumstances in which Europe found itself at the turn of the nineteenth century. It was in fact a response to the increasing subjectivization of western culture – the process by which what previously was considered to be objective reality came to be understood as the result of subjective choices. This itself must be seen as the result of the progressive disintegration of an order of objective certainty embodied in Christendom. As someone remarked: "In the 17th century men believed in Christianity, in the 18th they renounced and extirpated it and in the 19th they looked at it pathetically, gazing at it from the outside as one looks at an object in a museum."

Comte's most renowned successor in France was Emile Durkheim. Durkheim's *Rules of Sociological Method* is an outstanding exemplar of objectivism.[3] And now I introduce the term in its 'ismic' form, as an ideology that has so totally encompassed western thought that it is like the air we breathe: it has become both ubiquitous and impalpable. For Durkheim, if sociology is to be a distinct and autonomous discipline (on a par with other sciences), it is necessary to establish the prior existence of a realm or aspect of reality distinct and autonomous from other orders of reality. Also, it is essential to show that there exists a specifically scientific, i.e., objective knowledge of the social order with its own methods and forms of social explanation. As is well known, Durkheim used analogies from chemistry to show that when elements combine, a new type of existent compound results that often possesses properties that none of its elements individually possess. We know these as emergent properties: they take on a life of their own. Thus, it is unsurprising that Durkheim argued for the autonomy of social facts not only as objective but even as coercive.

What of the method of science? Durkheim explains: "Science goes from without, from the external and immediately sensible manifestations, to the interior characteristics of which these manifestations betray the existence."[4] Thus, Durkheim created the space for concepts such as social solidarity, collective conscience, anomie and the like. The facticity of the social demands "that the sociologist put himself in the same state of mind as the physicist, chemist or physiologist when he probes into a still unexplored realm of the scientific domain. When he penetrates the social world he must be aware that he is penetrating the unknown; he must feel himself in the presence of facts whose laws are as unsuspected as were those of life before the era of biology".[5]

Durkheim died in 1917, but in most social scientific circles he is mighty alive yet. He is the sociologist of order and consensus, a functionalist for whom all conflict or disorder is but a symptom of the failure of the system. For Durkheim, the norm and the normal is the average as it exists; the deviant is morbid or pathological. Though his methodological views appear to have passed into history, the world-view that underpins them is very much with us.

Durkheim's name is associated with both Positivism and Functionalism. Indeed, the latter is the true heir of the former. The term 'positive' for Comte had at least two central implications: on the one hand it referred to the certain kind of knowledge certified by science; on the other, it was the opposite of the negative, that is of the critical and destructive ideas of the French Revolution. The fact is that insofar as the 'positive' implied an emphasis upon the importance of scientifically certified knowledge, it could be exploited as a rhetoric that might provide a basis for certainty of belief and consensus in society. Durkheim's theory displayed the same fascination with cohesion and social consensus, and objectivity was the taproot of both. But Durkheim lived in an age in which modern industrial society was far more developed than it had been when Comte created positivism. The danger was no longer seen as located in vestigial institutions of the past, but more fully rooted in the present.

The thrust of Durkheim's work indeed shifted from economic poverty to the poverty of morality that he saw as rooted in the inherent insatiability of man. Durkheim rejected socialism, even progress. His was the problem of order, and the implicit slogan of the Functionalism to which he subscribed was "survival implies ongoing usefulness – search it out". Thus was the marriage of Functionalism and Utilitarianism consummated in sociology. The child of this union was a detached objectivity that denied intrinsic value attachments to objects, especially as they impeded buying and selling in an accelerating market economy. Gouldner's poignant observation is still meaningful today – especially to us:

> "...whether men keep or sell any object depends ultimately on the price offered for it. If they will sell themselves their time and their services for a price, there are few things they will balk at selling when the price is right. In such a culture there is therefore less of a strain in the demand that men be 'objective'."

An apparent contradiction appears here. We said that morality was high on Durkheim's agenda, yet he is a recognized functionalist. Can morality be viewed as functional? The answer is 'yes'. For Durkheim, the significance of moral values is primarily social: they contribute to social solidarity and the integration of the individual into an ongoing social order.

Durkheim's objectivistic rationale for morality would of course have been anathema to Max Weber, who saw its essential justification in the *meaning* that it endowed the life of individuals. Weber was heir to German Romanticism and Neo-Kantianism. But he lived in a world already conquered by science. As is well known, it was the overriding concern of not a few of his predecessors, notably Dilthey and Rickert, to work out the relation between the *naturwissenschaften* and the *geisteswissenschaften*.

For Weber, the problem of values and of the kind of understanding is unique to the cultural sciences, viz., interpretative understanding demanded resolution in what must be a coherent scientific methodology. His famous definition of sociology encapsulates his unique manner of resolving the issue: "Sociology is a science which attempts the interpretative understanding of social action in order thereby to arrive at a causal explanation of its course and effects."[7]

Sociology was to be at once value relevant and value free. Weber emphatically insisted that "an attitude of moral indifference has no connection with scientific 'objectivity'".[8] At the same time Weber rhetorically asked: "What is the validity of the value judgments which are uttered by the critic...? In what sense, if the criterion of scientific knowledge is to be found in the 'objective' validity of its results, has he remained within the sphere of *scientific* discussion?"[9] Weber's own problem was, in his own words: "In what sense are there in general 'objectively valid truths in those disciplines concerned with social and cultural phenomena?"[10] His answer came in terms of an ends-means analysis of all social phenomena. About the instrumental rationality he said: "All serious reflection about the ultimate elements of meaningful human conduct is oriented primarily in terms of the categories 'end' and 'means'. We desire something concretely either for its own sake, or as a means of achieving something else which is more highly desired. The question of the appropriateness of the means for achieving a given end is undoubtedly accessible to scientific analysis."[11] Thus a cost-benefit analysis so widely accepted today was proposed by Weber as the sole point of contact between human ends and means. For science strives merely for an 'analytical ordering of empirical reality! As he said: "It can never be the task of an empirical science to provide binding norms and ideals from which directives for immediate practical activity can be derived."

'Objectivity' for Weber was of course just another word for value freedom. And the touchstone of objectivity appears to be that a "correct scientific proof in the social sciences, if it is to achieve its purpose, must be acknowledged as correct even by a Chinese..."[12] Again, he argues that to the extent that it is scientific, a journal "should be a place where those truths are sought, which... can claim, even for a Chinese, the validity appropriate to an analysis of empirical reality".[13] So great was Weber's faith in the objectivity of scientific explanation! In fact, it is of some interest to note, in the context in which we speak, that despite his definition of social action in terms of the subjective meaning attached to it by the actor, and his avowed methodological individualism, Weber's researches objectified meanings on an unprecedented scale. Raymond Aron points out that in the *Protestant Ethic and the Spirit of Capitalism,* Protestantism "transcends individual consciousness; it was never lived in this way by any individual... If then the meaning which corresponds to the internal logic of conduct is already objective and not subjective, then Weber, without intending to, has created a science of objective meanings".[14] Aron's comment is of course aimed at Weber's well-known methodological meta-construct of Ideal Types.

Yet, Weber realized that it is not that it should be possible, but it is *necessary* that there be scientific criticism of ideals and value judgments. Such criticism will be *technical* in intent. Even when a judgment is involved, "it can be no more than a formal logical judgment of historically given value-judgments and ideas, a testing of the ideals according to the postulate of the internal consistency of the desired end."[15] For, "The fate of an epoch which has eaten of the tree of knowledge is that it must know that we cannot learn the *meaning* of the world from the results of its analysis, be it ever so perfect; it must rather be in a position to create this meaning itself".[16]

Thus did Weber make the split between the individual value-relating, meaning constructing subject of the specialized cultural sciences and the disenchanted, devalued, objective and meaningless world. This split is not given *a priori*; it is the product of history. Man has built his iron cage and is now condemned to live in it. From the Absolute Spirit of Hegel and even Dithery, continually realizing itself in the historical process, Weber's is indeed a far cry. For him history has ended; what alone remains is human responsibility.

We must now move away from mainstream social science to another tradition of social thought that bears the name of Karl Marx. Weber's stress on the autonomy of ideas was part of his debate with the ghost of Marx. It is difficult to summarize Marx without parodying him, largely because too many interpretations exist that, in fact, are parodies of his thought. To stay with the subject of objectivity (sic!), for Marx, it is social relations that underpin all of social reality – not the meaningful actions of individuals, nor the conscience collective. To quote: "The whole character of a species... is contained in the character of its life activity. The object of labour is therefore the objectification of man's species life."[17]

The key-concept in Marx's discourse, which is also the most complex, is, from the present point of view, that of *ideology*. The point to be stressed here is that ideology is not reducible to an error of perception, but arises rather from an accurate perception of how things represent themselves to experience. It is not the subject who deceives himself, but reality which deceives him. The mystifying mechanism, in other words, is an objective one, analogous to that which produces a mirage. Thus a false reality may nevertheless quite objectively confront men in their everyday experience. Marx distances himself from the philistines' and vulgar economists' way of looking at things because (as he says), "It is only the direct form of manifestation of relations that is reflected in their brains and not their inner connection".[18] Elsewhere he says: "all science would be superfluous if the outward appearance and the essence of things directly coincided"[19]

Recall Durkheim's superficially similar, but in essence diametrically opposed, statement that we earlier quoted. There Durkheim had claimed that "we can know causes scientifically only by the effects" and that "science chooses from these effects only the most objective and most easily measurable". For Marx, science is nothing if not critical. It must find place not so much for validity as for contradiction, not so much for a true objectivity predicated of consensus and social solidarity, but for the false objectivities, the reifications born of the conflict of mutually inconsistent symbolic universes. No doubt these false objectivities too have validity, but this they retain only under the conditions in which they are produced. Marx's trenchant critique of political economy sought to expose the fallacy of its supposition that its categories are eternal and universal in their application. Indeed, in the larger historical scheme, Marx emphasized again and again, the rationale of the capitalist state, for only in bourgeois society does total alienation, the *sine qua non* of the revolutionary consciousness, exists. Therein lie at once its phenomenal rationality, its fundamental irrationality and its historical rationale.

It is impossible to do justice to the complexities of Marx's thought. And it is something of a struggle with ideas to encompass Marx's meaning when he says: "An objective being... would not act objectively if the quality of objectivity did not reside in the very nature of his being. He creates, posits objects alone, *because* he is posited by objects – because at bottom he is nature".[20] Marcuse has developed this theme in the following way:

> The objective world, as the necessary objectivity of man, through the appropriation and suppression of which his human essence is first 'produced' and 'confirmed', is part of man himself. It is real objectivity only for self-realizing man; it is the 'self-objectification' of man, or human objectification. But this same objective world, since it is real objectivity, can appear as a precondition of his being which does not belong to his being, is beyond his control, and is 'overpowering'. This conflict in the human essence – that is in itself objective – is the root of the fact that objectification can become reification and that externalization can become alienation.

In denying a petrified and a historical notion of objectivity and rationality, Marx bequeathed a powerful tool of analysis to the social sciences. Its political implications, however, were such that Anglo-American social science has displayed only a phobic attitude towards it.

Eventually, and one might say, inevitably, the standard notion of objectivity collapsed within the natural sciences themselves, and when it did, there resulted a crisis of confidence in science, one with which the West and, of course, all of us in tow, still living.

Part II

If, for the social *sciences*, the question of objectivity has always been and continues to be a burning issue, for the natural sciences, objectivity has always appeared as the condition *sine qua non* of science itself. As Jacques Monod put it in *Chance and Necessity*: "The postulate of objectivity is substantial with science and has guided the whole of its prodigious development for three centuries. It is impossible to escape it, even provisionally, or in a limited area, without departing from science itself".[22] In fact, it is because of the widespread acceptance of this view regarding science *per se* that the problem of the status of the social sciences (dealing as they must with the subjects of belief, intention and action) has loomed so large and has even forced some thinkers today to reject the very idea of a *social science*.

During the second half of the 20th century, however, there has appeared a powerful critique of the notion of objectivity in the philosophy of natural science itself. This critique has taken many forms. Quite understandably, these forms correspond to the many forms that objectivity has itself taken: objectivity as facticity, as consensus; objectivity as value freedom, objectivity as truth, even infallibility and not the least, objectivity as the rationality of scientific method.

Richard Rorty spells these ideas out in the following way: "In our culture, the notions of 'science', 'rationality', 'objectivity', and truth are bound up with one another. Science is thought of as offering 'hard' 'objective' truth: truth as correspondence to reality the only sort of truth worthy of the mere Humanists – for example philosophers, theologians, historians and literary critics – have to worry about whether they are being 'scientific', whether they are entitled to think of their conclusions, no matter how carefully argued, as worthy of the term 'true'. We tend to identify seeking 'objective truth' with 'using reason' and so we think of the natural sciences as paradigms of rationality. We also think of rationality as a matter of following procedures laid down in advance, of being methodical. So we tend to use 'methodical' 'rational' 'scientific' and 'objective as synonyms".[23] Indeed, he goes on to say: "The roots of scientism, defined as the view that rationality is a matter of applying criteria, is the desire for objectivity, the hope that ... human flourishing has a transhistorical nature."[24]

In this article, Rorty himself argues for a toning down of the notion of the 'rational' to mean no more than reasonable, undogmatic, and persuasive rather than coercive. On this interpretation, of course, there ceases to be any special problem for the social sciences as distinct from the natural. Further, in so far as these terms are synonymous, the problem of objectivity, for Rorty at least, stands dissolved rather than resolved. Solidarity is the new incumbent.

But we must go somewhat further back to those accounts of science that prompted these fulminations in the first place. And whereas one should start from the advent of Logical Positivism and the claim of the members of the Vienna Circle that the edifice of science rests on the infallible bedrock of sense data (note the irony of turning the quintessentially subjective sense data into the objective basis of science), I will assume that this is familiar terrain which does not require to be traversed again.

Karl Popper's scathing critique of Radical Empiricism sought objectivity first in the hypothetico-deductive method of testing, what finer guarantor of objectivity could there be than logic, and later in the well known notion of the objective third world of ideas, theories and even of problem, puzzles and intelligibles. Moreover, in Popper's view, even the empathetic understanding of other people's actions (he refers here to Collingwood's reenactment thesis) "consists, essentially in operating with third-world objects". This world and its objects may indeed be the product of human activity. Recall that it consists of theories, problems etc. But it develops an autonomy; it transcends its makers. It contains information but also misinformation, solutions but also questions. Popper himself likens the contents of this world to Fregean 'objective thought contents'. In this manner, Popper combines an ontological objectivism with an epistemological fallibilism.

In the social sciences, Popper's epistemology finds its counterpart in situational logic. Here, though the 'situation' must be defined in terms of the actors' beliefs, aims and individual limitations, logic ensures an objective evaluation and indeed explanation of social action/institutions. One of Popper's key-statements around which indeed a large debate exists can serve as a take-off point for what is known as the sociology of science. Popper says: "We should realize that the study of the products [of knowledge] is vastly more important than the study of the production, even for an understanding of the production and its methods."[25] We will return to this at the end of this lecture. For the moment we proceed somewhat sequentially to the views of Popper's eminent pupil Imre Lakatos.

Note that, after Popper's hard-hitting critique of Empiricism, the notion of scientific truth had to retire hurt. The player in was variously called verisimilitude, corroboration, confirmation and the like. But rationality still reigned supreme. However in responding to the forceful arguments of Thomas Kuhn, Lakatos himself conceded that there is no instant rationality in science. The arguments and case studies contained in his major paper *The Methodology of Scientific Research Programmes* cannot be summarized here.[26] The point we wish to focus on is that since the work of Kuhn and Lakatos, the history of science as historiography has come to live in permanently with the philosophy of science. In an important sense, it was Karl Popper who opened the door that made this possible, but he also stood firmly astride in front, barring the entry of any outsiders. In denying instant rationality, Lakatos was really denying the possibility of a crucial experiment in science which would permit the scientific community to unanimously accept one theory rather than another, because of results from which unequivocal conclusions could be drawn. It is well known that what for Popper appeared in his meta-theory as the notion of refutation was belied by the actual history of science. Thus, Lakatos recognized that the scientific community could live with inconsistency in the theoretical network for considerable periods of time, dismissing it as a mere temporary anomaly, i.e. as a problem that will find resolution as research progresses.

When does an anomaly turn into an actual counter-example, even refuting evidence of a theory? When the research programme begins to degenerate, when it ceases to provide insightful explanations or to make useful predictions, in other words, when it ceases to be progressive. At that point, it is rational to reject the entire programme. In fact, Lakatos goes one step further when he argues that so long as a group of scientists does not fool itself about the track record of the research programme in which it chooses to work, it is rational even to cling to a degenerating research programme. How is this so? The answer again is called from the history of science that teaches us that important scientific ideas may suffer great vicissitudes of fortune that a degenerating programme can, and in fact, has become, progressive after a lapse of some centuries. Take the case of the heliocentric hypothesis. Aristarchus in the history of science proposed it much before Copernicus. This goes to show that the process of the growth of scientific knowledge is amenable to rational reconstruction, i.e. its rationality is discernible and describable only after the event. This was a major concession, but Lakatos, in turn, insisted on the distinction between the rational internal history of science and its external (possibly irrational) history, that, as he insisted, must only find place in the footnotes!

Thomas Kuhn's *The Structure of Scientific Revolutions* is a many faceted work, widely cited, discussed and critiqued.[27] We will, in this paper, concentrate on Kuhn's somewhat complex notion of objectivity. Kuhn rejected the notion of rationality as method guided by the light of objective criteria. Not even mainstream philosophers of science, he notes, "have claimed to possess either a complete or an entirely well-articulated list of criteria." "For some time" he continues, "they could reasonably expect that further research would ... produce an algorithm able to dictate a rational unanimous choice. Pending that achievement, scientists would have no alternative but to supply subjectively what the best current list of objective criteria still lacked".[28] (Note the air of paradox in the phrase 'current list of objective criteria'). No philosopher of science, says Kuhn, now seriously expects a decision procedure in the natural sciences.

One way of saving the objectivity of science was, as we have seen, to distinguish sharply between the psychology of discovery and the logic of the justification of scientific hypotheses. But such a distinction goes violently against the history of actual scientific practice. For, what is used today, typically through textbooks, to justify the acceptance of a theory, more often than not, was no part of the 'evidence' that influenced scientists individually or collectively in the choice of theory at the time of its first appearance. As Kuhn argues, "that choice was made on the basis of a curious mixture of the 'objective' situation and subjective preferences which finally persuaded the community as a whole. Thus, the choices scientists make between competing theories depend not only on shared criteria – those my critics call objective – but also on idiosyncratic factors dependent on individual biography and personality".[29] If this is true for physics – and let us remind ourselves that it is a once practising scientist who speaks – then how much more vulnerable are the social sciences dealing with societies, one's' own and alien, to the vagaries of the researchers' biography and personality? How much more is at stake in claims about the behavior of our kith and kin, of the members of our own culture than in claims about the behavior of alpha particles!

Indeed, Kuhn makes an even subtler point when he says: "If subjective factors are required to account for the decisions that initially divide the profession, they may still be present later when the profession agrees".[30] Kuhn alludes here to the entire system of cognitive values that vary not only from discipline to discipline but also in the course of time. In fact, the marriage of the history and philosophy of science in Kuhn's work is clearly transformed into a *menage a trois* with sociology becoming a major partner. Thus, even though the *form* of the cognitive values that Kuhn recognizes, such as accuracy, consistency, scope, simplicity and fruitfulness, are the ones he shares with hardheaded epistemologists as the permanent attributes of science, he insists that "little knowledge of history is required to suggest that both the application of these values and, more obviously, the relative weight attached to them have varied markedly with time and also with the field of application."[31] Further, Kuhn argues that two sets of cognitive values can in their application contradict each other that makes relative weighing necessary, which again is a subjective matter. Such a situation "requires a decision processes that permits rational men to disagree' which further ensures that the scientific tradition is never petrified."[32] Note the phrase 'rational men to disagree'...

Kuhn has been accused of irrationalism and of seeing theory choice as a matter of mob psychology. He has pleaded 'not guilty' to both charges. Yet, the idea of a social consensus which we met with in discussing Durkheim and which philosophers such as Richard Rorty refer to as solidarity, plays an important though convoluted role in his understanding of objectivity. Such is the subjectivity of scientific objectivity!

In the last section of this paper, we take a look at the out and out sociology of science position as formulated by Barnes and Bloor – best known as the Strong Programme. Bloor puts the position succinctly when he says, "epistemic factors are really social factors". Does this vitiate their truth/rationality? The symmetry thesis of the Strong Programme states that social factors operate indiscriminately in all knowledge situations – true or false. Moreover, the reflexivity thesis states that the strong programme is itself amenable to sociological analysis. Thus, whereas Kuhn would go no further than stating the fact, for instance, that Descartes' emphasis on clear and distinct ideas must be understood as Descartes understood and applied them, Bloor goes on to insist that the further problem that awaits us is: 'how and why was the principle applied the way it was?' Which of course has no bearing on the question: Was Descartes right to think of extension as a clear and distinct idea? Thus, in general, one must say that social factors come to the fore in explaining why particular implications were constructed in the way they were, and why different groups construed these implications differently.

This position is of course in sharp contrast to that of Popper, for whom, as we noted earlier, only the product of the knowledge machine, not the process, is of any interest. Quite understandably, Bloor directly attacks Popper in his paper 'A Sociological Theory of Objectivity'.[33] Here, as he himself claims, he seeks to show that Popper's Third World is really the social world. Further, that without being aware of it, Popper is really describing the status and character of a social institution. Popper's ontology requires demystification. Thus Popper's claim of 'epistemology without a knowing subject' can and should be understood as the knowledge that belongs to the collectivity. This idea is somewhat reminiscent of Durkheim's social facts.

Popper's claim of autonomy for the Third World rests largely on the assumption that logic operates on data and, by itself generates more and more objective data irrespective of whether any human being has drawn those implications. But any social theory of objectivity makes the usual talk about implications and consequences look problematic. For, it would have to be built on the idea that our talk about 'discovering' the implications of our assertions really covers up an act of *creation*. In other words, logical necessity is not a universal or an absolute. In Bloor's words, "logical implications do not pre-exist: we construct them as we go along depending on nothing but the dispositions that we possess naturally, or have been given in the course of our training." This view is not unfamiliar, since, in the history of logic, it has been strongly defended by the Intuitionists. Thus the widely held belief that logical implications do pre-exist, itself calls for special sociological explanation! Now it might be argued, that in drawing implications from premises, we must always follow a rule that at least is precise in its import. But, argues Bloor, the meaning of a rule is itself a highly problematic notion. Meanings are not created once and for all; they are continually created and recreated. As Wittgenstein famously put it, "no course of action could be determined by a rule, because every course of action can be made to accord with the rule".

Thus two belief systems have different ways of synthesizing information and processing experience. If so, then we may reasonably speak of different kinds of objectivity and science itself must be seen as a belief system, subscribing to its own and *changing* set of objective truths. It is no more, no less.

We appear now to have come full circle to where we began this exercise. The social sciences sought their paradigm in the methods of the natural sciences. Their objectivity was to be scientific objectivity. At the end of the day, we are confronted with the strong argument that scientific objectivity is in fact social. So where do we go from here?

Notes

1. Habermas, J., *Knowledge and Human Interests*, Translated by Jeremy J. Shapiro, Boston, 1971, p. 71.
2. Quoted in Ted Benton, *Philosophical Foundations of Three Sociologies*, London, 1977, p. 202.
3. Translated and edited by S.A. Salovay and J.H. Meuller, Illinois, 1950.
4. "Individual and Collective Representations." Reprinted in *Sociology and Philosophy*, New York, 1974, p. 19.
5. Durkheim, E., *Rules of Sociological Method*, "Author's Introduction", p. xlv. *Op cit.*
6. Gouldner, A., *The Coming Crisis of Western Sociology*, London, 1972, p. 102.
7. Weber, M., *The Theory of Social and Economic Organization*, Edited by Talcott Parsons, New York, 1947, p. 88.
8. *Max Weber on the Methodology of Social Sciences*, Translated and edited by Edward A. Shils and Henry A. Finch, Illinois, 1949, p. 60.
9. *Max Weber on the Methodology of Social Sciences, Op cit.*, pp. 50-51.
10. *Max Weber on the Methodology, Op cit.*, p. 63.
11. *Max Weber on the Methodology, Op cit.*, p. 65.
12. *Max Weber on the Methodology of Social Sciences, Op cit.*, p. 58.
13. *Max Weber on the Methodology of Social Sciences, Op cit.*, p. 59.
14. *Main Currents of Sociological Thought*, Vol. 2, London, 1967, p. 209.
15. Weber, Max, "Objectivity in Social Sciences and Social Policy," in *Values, Objectivity and the Social Sciences*, Edited by Gresham Riley, Reading, 1974, p. 73.
16. Weber, Max, "Objectivity in Social Sciences and Social Policy," *Op cit.*, p. 76.
17. Marx, Karl, "First Manuscript: Alienated Labour," in *Karl Marx: Early Writings*, Edited by T.B. Bottomore, New York, 1963, p. 127.
18. Marx, Karl, "First Manuscript: Alienated Labour," *Op cit*, p. 128.
19. Marx, Karl, *The Capital*, Vol. 3, Moscow, 1972, p. 83.

20. Marx, Karl, "The Third Manuscript: Critique of Hegel's Dialectic," in *Karl Marx: Early Writings, Op cit.*, p. 206.
21. Marcuse, H., *One-Dimensional Man: Studies in the Ideology of Advanced Industrial Society*, Boston, 1964, p.18.
22. London, 1971, p. 39.
23. Rorty, R., "Objectivity or Solidarity" in his *Objectivity, Relativism and Truth*, Cambridge, 1991, p. 35.
24. Rorty, "Objectivity or Solidarity", p.27.
25. Popper, Karl, *Objective Knowledge: An Evolutionary Approach*, Oxford, 1972, p. 114.
26. Cambridge, 1978.
27. Chicago, 1972.
28. Kuhn, Thomas, "Objectivity, Judgment and Theory Choice" in his *The Essential Tension: Selected Studies in Scientific Tradition and Change*, Chicago, 1977, p. 326.
29. Objectivity, Value Judgment and Theory Choice," *Op cit.*, p. 329.
30. Ibid.
31. "Objectivity, Value Judgment and Theory Choice", *Op cit.*, p. 335.
32. "Objectivity, Value Judgement and Theory Choice", *Op cit.*, p. 332.
33. See S.C. Brown (ed.), *Objectivity and Cultural Change*, Cambridge, 1981, pp. 229-245.

3

History, Hermeneutics and Methodological Objectivity

RAJAN GURUKKAL

History is not any more an account of kings, their genealogies, wars they fought and treaties made. Just as any other social science, history today also seeks to explain social phenomena. Historians may be specific about the aspects of their specialization, but they know that no area of inquiry ever exists in a pure state with the desired exclusiveness. The aspects of collective human life are interrelated. It is no longer possible to do history partitioned into social, economic, cultural, political, religious, etc. as independent facets. Facets do continue and may be important, but not anymore as part of the logical processes of thought formation. It is solely a strategy of classification and intended for better communication. The totality is taken for granted even in specializing a narrow aspect of social processes.

The task of the modern historian is not just to describe the events in their chronological, sequential order but primarily to conceive the events as a process and reach out to the phenomena through explanation. It is a *hermeneutical* project. Much more than being concerned about what has happened, the historian seeks to know the *nature* of happenings. What *kind* of happenings, *how* and *why*, rather than *when* and *where*, they have happened, are the essential preliminaries that now define the historical problematic. Such an agenda of inquiries leads to an interpretative production of knowledge, through a process of analytical discoveries of correlations and a priori reasoning, amongst apparently disconnected aspects of social life. It is an intellectual exercise that demands enormous methodological rigour.

Methodology is often discussed merely as a set of methods or techniques in the academic circles, especially in the context of graduating students as researchers. It is true that the term literally means the 'science of research methods.' But what is being increasingly neglected is the aspect of logical construct or the role of the explanatory framework. Historical methodology's most vital aspect is the study of explanatory frameworks that are conceptual tools for understanding phenomena. When historians think seriously, they think conceptually, and that has been the practice ever since the inception of methodology in doing history. In fact, it was not European historiography that illustrated the conceptual dimension for the first time, but it could be found in the works of Ibn Khaldun way back in the fourteenth century.[1] *Mukhadimmah* was the first serious historical work on historical methodology ever written with theoretical insights into the past. Khaldunian's perspectives hardly go beyond West Asia due to obvious reasons. Even the countries in the neighbourhood had not heard of *Mukhadimmah* until European historiographers began referring to them.

Theoretical discussions on history became significant with the writings of the German philosopher Hegel. The theory acquired the rigour of a mature science in the Historical

Materialism of Marx, the major transforming influence of western historiography till date. Materialistic interpretation of history, as formulated by Marx, has no fixed ends, it is a continuously growing science of historical explanation. The primary position of Marxian methodology as the major totalizing theory of history goes as yet unchallenged in spite of the fact that there have been alternative frameworks of and supplementary formulations for the materialistic methodology. In the current academic parlance, totalizing theories are called 'grand theories' or meta-narratives that as a *genre* has gone somewhat obsolete. But for more than a century, the grand theory of Marxism has been the most vital current in the hermeneutic activity of historians. The Marxist teleology made history a challenging discipline of hermeneutical research.

Hermeneutics is a decoding exercise in unraveling the underlying correlations in a social process. It is an analytical strategy for the syntactic decipherment of social phenomena. Under the general rubric of hermeneutics, social scientists and philosophers generate meanings through varying modes of interpretations as we gather from the deeper syntactic inquiries of Schleiermacher, the father of scientific hermeneutics, and Dilthey, Heidegger, Garfinkel and Taylor. The Schleiermacherian variety of hermeneutics is an interpretative technique with which Christianity recuperated its scriptures and spiritual activities, and the fundamental meaning as eschatological idea or essence. Dilthey, in a broader sense, taking its cue from the Greek times, defined hermeneutics as the science that developed the laws of interpretation.[2] He believed that hermeneutical subjection of human objectifications, i.e., the relics of human articulations in language, literature, and writing, would unveil the spirit of history, *verstehen*. Hermeneutics was his main strategy of comprehension governing the process of understanding history through long drawn-out reflection on the nature of *verstehen.* He aimed at reaching, through his hermeneutical approach, the fundamental level of collective human life in order to reconstruct its foundational science. His concept of *verstehen* signifies an interpretative project of universal validity that Garfinkel's *Sociology* and Charles Taylor's *Political Science* explicitly vouch for.

Whatever one thinks, there is no doubt that the historical knowledge owed its exponential growth not to the exhaustive compilation of data on the past, but to the critical syntactic practice based on hermeneutics. The hermeneutical project of history necessitates historians to possess at least a resonance of all major conceptual formulations about social processes. No process/phenomenon as such does imply any discipline-based identity. It is our approach that makes it so. A serious historian is therefore constrained to be aware of the exponential wisdom in every social science. For a long time we believed, and many of us still believe, that history written by great historians of the past is final and conceptions propounded by them are universal. Today, after many a year the old methods, concepts, and terminology of history have phased out substantially, and several times the ways of perceiving the past and expressing it have changed over decades. We continue to see that historical interpretations, proclaimed as ultimate resolutions to many a problem, suddenly lose their significance and get abandoned.

Nevertheless, there is a store of lasting hermeneutical wealth behind the dissolving concepts and theories, providing contemporary foundations of historical knowledge. A professionally committed historian will have to imbibe this epistemologically significant dimension about social sciences.[3] However old be the society he/she concentrates upon, it is impossible to conceive it without a social scientific perspective in which the orthodox contours and boundaries of disciplines get merged.[4] A historian is a social scientist as well.[5] The field of historical inquiry today is as much descriptively horizontal and sectoral as interpretatively vertical and temporal. It is the most potent discipline that tends to transcend its conventional boundaries and stake the claim of being an interdisciplinary domain of knowledge. As Roland Barthes wrote:

> Interdisciplinary work, so much discussed these days, is not about confronting already constituted disciplines (none of which, in fact, is willing to let itself go.) To do something interdisciplinary it is not enough to choose a 'subject' (a theme) and gather around it two or three sciences. Interdisciplinarity consists in creating a new object that belongs to no one.

Interdisciplinarity involves the practice of a different mode of perception with which the usual historiography is not quite familiar. The perception extricates an object of knowledge from the limiting influence of discipline-based pin-hole vision which keeps us blind to the larger world surrounding it. Many a theme of knowledge unencumbered by the techniques of existing disciplines does emerge in the process that might even lead to the making of new epistemologies. An immediate impact of interdisciplinary perspective is the increasing awareness about the radical shift in the nature of knowledge, amounting to putting the last first or getting determinants made determined and vice versa.

As for the discipline of history, the act of doing history has emerged as the most profound of all its interdisciplinary objects. What necessitates history and what makes knowledge possible are being seriously discussed now with better insights into the question as to why history gets re-written from time to time. There was a strong feeling that the act of redoing history of the one and the same spatio-temporal specificity not only aimed at, but also attained, higher and higher levels of objectivity. But it is hard to find any well-informed historian of our times who is led by such a courage of hoping to be more and more objective in the process.

The objectivity-claim in the Rankeyean approach or the Buryan scientific history is no longer a pretension of historical methodology today. The kind of objectivity that a historian can talk about now is related to the strategies ensuring the most honest self-criticism within the hermeneutic activity. Objectivity lies in the method of self-scrutiny and in the confession of historians that helps appropriate evaluation within the limitations of their hermeneutics. The objective knowledge is concerned about the possibility of empirically verifiable primary experience and not about the basis of the possibility of such knowledge itself.[7] The self-reflexivity theory of practice puts objective knowledge back on its feet by showing concern about what conditions make such knowledge possible. In historical studies, the term objectivity should be used as a metaphor to indicate the methodological strategies of self-scrutiny.

What is objective about a historian's practice is his/her commitments to advancing knowledge about the past – the commitments to the task of looking for data that nullify the foundational theory of the hypothesis under test.[8] It is the possibility of critical assessment, including criticism of the act of assessment, within hermeneutics, that makes history scientific. So the crucial question would be: how spacious would be one's hermeneutical range of self-criticism for facilitating reciprocity between the mental process of idealism and the physical process of verification. The scientific characteristic of the whole enterprise of a historian is ensured not by the new ideas s/he discovers, but by his/her methodological self-reflexivity to check their veracity.

History, like any other discipline, is a body of knowledge with its own rules of formulation. There are certain common characteristics about these rules, notwithstanding the controversy over what these common characteristics are, let alone what they should be. The orthodox among historians would assert that undoubtedly the significant characteristic of history is objectivity. To them, historical literature by and large satisfies, in general terms, all the normal criteria of scientific knowledge. But that is not enough to call the discipline objective. How can a subject-matter whose object is alienable, intractable and reacting, be made objective? Historical knowledge is the result of enactments in the historians' minds that never succeed in escaping the influence of affective response, however methodologically inclined they are, to inquire 'how it works' rather than 'what it means.' Human affairs that historians seek to reconstruct are not spectacles to be seen dispassionately, but experiences to be lived through in their own minds. It is indeed a subjective exercise for them because of the dimension of purposive action and the value-impregnated aspect unavoidable in doing history. In fact, subjectivity is the strength of historical studies that necessitate non-objective techniques of investigation. A historical exercise acquires enormous explanatory potential when the historian dares to project himself or herself empathetically into the historical phenomena. "Rigorous sciences can never be neutral in human affairs; attempts to put oneself outside of history at best produce rigorous pseudo-sciences like logic."[9]

In the above sense, can history ever be a scientific discipline? A scientific discipline is vested with explanatory potential enabling the discovery of laws governing the phenomena under study. This provides the discipline with the capacity to predict. Ever since their inception, the aim of social sciences has always been to explain social phenomena and formulate their laws. But the aim remains unattained as yet. All social sciences, including history, have failed in their attempts at making law-like generalizations, and naturally they are weak in making predictions. History does explain human affairs and social processes, but it does not entail the discovery of laws. However, there is no logical impossibility or *reductio ad absurdum* proof to show that social phenomena are unpredictable. J.B. Bury, following Pascal, once suggested, in his famous essay "Cleopatra's Nose," that the possibility of counterfactual reconstruction in the form of agglutinative causation of an historical event cannot be ignored. He wrote: "The cause of the foundation of Roman empire was the length of Cleopatra's nose; had her features been imperfectly proportioned, Mark Antony would not have been entranced; had he not been entranced, he would not have allied himself with Egypt against Octavian; had he not made alliance, the Battle of Actium would not have been fought and so on."[10]

Such game-theoretic situations apart, it is of utmost importance to highlight that social phenomena are far more complicated than natural physical phenomena. Social processes are extremely complex and subtle. Every aspect of them is unique and beyond the sphere of scientific investigation and formulation of laws. Social prediction is to depend on factors that are numerous, intractable, culturally contingent, and frequently varying. Anything that is potent of radical conceptual innovation precludes predictability. Even in the material sciences prediction is possible only in areas like thermodynamics. But there is no science enabling prediction of the future of thermodynamics. "Just as no one could predict quantum mechanics or special relativity, no one could have predicted Luther's distinctive doctrine of justification or the first elaboration of Kant's theory of knowledge. Any aspect of social life is like this. There are always radical conceptual innovations about it. Hence systematically unpredictable."[11]

But just as in the physical sciences, none of the innovations in social sciences is inexplicable and as usual every scientific explanation succeeds the innovation. Explanation presupposes theorization, but not as objectively as in physical sciences. Theoretical production in social sciences does not, however, take place in abstraction, but results from incessant interaction between experiencing and conceptualization. Theorization of a historical process is never based on the restoration of reality about it in any absolute form. It is a logical abstraction of historically real differences into a theoretically plausible unity. Theories in history are logical constructs, often made up of imaginary relations based on facts of greater or lesser veracity, either way leaving knowledge about the past phenomena incomplete. Though it is reflection and speculation that pave the ground for theory construction, the theory, once constructed, is thrown open in the grid of methodological evaluation that can critique from all directions, and pose new problems against theoretical conclusions. If verification has any meaning here, it lies in the open. The eternal vigilance exercised through reflective and speculative thought is the only immediate safeguard.

It is not possible to determine logically whether a theory is true or false beyond its own measures.[12] But it is relatively easy to assess its academic validity that is explicit in its structure as a cohesive framework of comprehension capable of generating new knowledge. A new theory rises not as the successful contender of a pre-existing one that gradually dies off in the minds of the people. A rising generation, deprived of the cumulative impact of the relegated theory, is familiarized with the new. It is a start afresh with a new generation. Each generation is committed to a paradigm, the rejection of which amounts to its loss of pattern of recognizing knowledge. As Thomas Kuhn says, the gestalt shift is fundamentally a psychological process which is non-rational.[13] The ascendancy of a new theory is not always through the logical processes of the breakdown of the pre-existing theory. Every new theory solves a puzzle that a pre-existing theory had failed to resolve and is more a feeling the paradigm imposes than real. New paradigms constitute new ways of conceiving puzzles and hence new modes of solving them.

It is true that even in the physical sciences theorization is the result of empirical process mediated by imagination. But it is incomparably different in the sense that in social sciences the empirical dimension is so weak, and bewilderingly varying, as to be hardly ever amenable to induction. Logically a domain that defies induction cannot be deductive in the strict sense either. So in history and other social sciences one can think of no theorization of the absolute type, but only conceptualizations of the hypothetico-deductive kind.

The particularizing concepts about the various social phenomena are numerous that can be called analytical tools of hypothetico-deductive approaches. The interdisciplinary social science methodology today comprises an extensive collection of conceptual tools and frameworks of comprehension such as Marxism, Critical Theory, Functionalism, Structuralism, Structuralist Marxism, Phenomenology, Substantivism, Semiology, Deconstruction, Discourse analysis, Narratology, Feminism, and Post-Modernism. A comprehensive study of historical methodology comprises lessons about all these meta-narratives and conceptual formulations, and these are explanatory tools of historians too. The modern way of practising hermeneutics in history demands at least a tenuous knowledge about these tools and an epistemological assessment of their validity. Of all the recently enunciated conceptual tools, 'discourse analysis' developed by Michel Foucault and the various other post-structuralist formulations rank foremost in the domain of historical interpretation as well as interpretation of interpretations.[14]

Michel Foucault used the term 'discourse' to signify a conceptual setting far beyond its usual semantic context. In the closest approximation to a definition, he would regard a discourse as groups of 'statements' belonging to the same 'discursive formation.' The terms 'statement' and 'discursive formations' mean new things to him. 'Statements', that form themselves as series, are 'historically produced statements authored by a group of spatio-temporaily and culturally related individuals or historically connected individuals.' A 'discourse' is constituted by a domain of meanings produced through a series of statements dispersed over the 'discursive formation' which is a broad semiotic space that makes statements possible. The number of statements possible in a discourse is unlimited. A discourse generates umpteen prescriptions, views, institutions, and programme. It covers the entire domain of human life, economy, culture, society, demography, health, education, planning and much else, giving the impression of a vast earning process and an extensive terrain of knowledge.

Discourse is knowledge the people mediate and seek about themselves. All knowledge is discursive knowledge enabling the exercise of power. It operates by mapping the social landscape, sculpting the economies, and transforming the cultures. There is no discourse-free knowledge that is produced and made available in the form of discursive texts. Discourse is a pattern of thinking for the recognition of truth. It shapes in significant ways the modes of social existence and rules social actions and designs. There is a fundamental level of description at which thought can be seen to be organized in a particular formation called discourse. The notion of discourse is meant to characterize, not just any formation in human knowledge, but a specific phenomenon that can be used to account for and to assess other formations. It is at once the hegemonic form of representation and the basis of redefining all representations.

A student of history will be interested to know about the formative processes of a discourse. Foucault resorts to tow his major conceptual formulations: (a) subjectification and (b) objectification – to explain how a discourse realizes itself. 'Subjectification' is the process of the making of the subject and 'objectification' the process of production of knowledge required for facilitating 'subjectification.' A discourse breaks down as a slow process, enabling shift of subjectivity through the operation of new discursive formations. In the words of Foucault: "A change in the order of discourse does not presuppose new ideas, a little invention and creativity, a different mentality, but transformations in a practice, perhaps also in neighboring practices, and in their common articulations."[15]

A discourse presupposes a subject position. The subjects maintain the discourse by being its subjects. Any era has its reigning discourse that governs the speech and action of the subjects. Since they speak and think within the rules of the reigning discourse, there is no possibility of knowing the discourse exhaustively. The rules, while providing them a vision, make them blind to other possible visions.

Since it is the discourse that shapes the modes of intellectual production, history, as it is written, is discursive. Then it is not the historian who deserves our attention but the discourse to which the historian's statements belong. This approach undermines the significance of individual historians and their supremacy though their causal roles in the discursive subjectification remain. The historian is only a function of the discourse that governs his/her intellectual practice.[16] So it hardly matters who is writing history, since the structure, composition, and meaning of what is written are discursive impositions. They form a part of the strategies of objectification under the reigning discourse. This is admittedly an indifferent approach to history and historiography, an approach palatable more to people with little history and historian's craft. But behind its cynical overtone, there is a deeper insight into the making of history by historians.

The philosophical justification of the discourse analysis is that "it enables to think reality differently, to learn to what extent the effort to think one's own history can free thought from what it silently thinks, and so to think differently." His analysis unravels the truth which people define themselves, but exactly as construed by others who are the progenitors of the discourse, and internalize that as truth about themselves. This enables us to discover that we see ourselves through the eyes of others without knowing that and without the ability to know that. There is a great deal of new knowledge available in the regime the analysis opens up. It gives a different dimension to the science of interpretation of interpretations. But the technique is useful more as a tool that strengthens self-reflexivity and self-criticism rather than as vital sources that regenerate theories. In spite of all methodological advantages of discourse-analysis in nuancing social phenomena, Marxism continues to be regarded as the most regenerative theory of social phenomena.

As Anderson has ably defended, historical materialism has distinctiveness as a critical theory leaving indivisibly and unremittingly enough scope for self-criticism in contrast to what is often mistakenly made out.[17] Marxism is still superior to all other accounts as a theory of historical development that lays claim, at the same stroke, to provide a theory of theory as well. Historical materialism remains the only paradigm to theorize the present as emerging from the structures of the past, as a rigorous theory of the distinctive dynamics of social development as a whole. There is a widespread feeling that it has become obsolete and has gone out of use from the scene of social scientific research. But this is primarily due to an unwarranted mixing up of the theory with the East European debacle of the Communist governments. Actually it is not the Marxist theory, but its political agenda that is deeply in crisis. This is not to say that all the explanatory pretensions of the theory go unchallenged, nor is it the case that there have been no substantial modifications of it. The core of the theory, i.e., its rational kernel, still remains the most successful contender of bourgeois theory and practice, when viewed in terms of its epistemological status. The hermeneutics one resorts to as a practising historian is to be based on this rational kernel that is Marx's theory of history.

Historical materialism as propounded in the *Formen* section of *Gundrisse* is a well-accomplished theory in itself.[18] It acquired further strength and cohesiveness through the later writings of Engels. On the one hand, it is a grand evolutionary narrative of massive, epochal transformation from one mode of production to another in the sequential order starting from primitive communism to slavery to feudalism to capitalism to communism. On the other hand, it is a compact theory – a theory of mode of production – of enormous potential as a rigorous instrument of micro level social analysis. It is the latter aspect of dexterity and finesse in explaining the forces of short-term changes that is epistemologically significant about the theory today. The theory is certainly a search for subjective agencies capable of effective strategies for the development of objective structures. What is much more significant is that these subjective agencies can be analyzed as objective structures, a methodological double-bind that substantiates the claim of Marxism to be a theory of theory.

Marxist hermeneutics is objective as long as its theoretical project for understanding the world is not marred by the political project of changing it. It is the methodological guard resisting the influence of normative Marxism that makes objectivity possible in the hermeneutic approach. Within this hermeneutic approach there is no sanctity attached to the canonical sequence of modes of production, nor categories like the Asiatic mode. Similarly, there is no sanctity of the nature of a mode of production's institutional features since they are unique and historically contingent. For instance, the feudal mode would require neither serfdom nor seigneurial power that are regionally specific institutional features. Therefore, the presence of institutional features would not help us determine the mode of production either. It is the processes and reactions that are decisive.

Marxist hermeneutics presents a distinct interpretative strategy that is immensely generative of new knowledge, even though in its mechanical doctrinaire fashion it seems to lead us hardly beyond theoretical empiricism. But it is caught up in certain fundamental issues around the basic genre history that is noted for its allegorical and dramatizing characteristics. It constitutes a story telling mode in which the exploits of individual heroes, rulers, administrators, and other important personages are represented. Such an ideographic exercise cannot satisfy even the preliminary heuristic interest of the hermeneutical agenda. Moreover, the heuristic approach is highly analytical and proceeds with conceptual categories like classes, structures, institutions, and ideas than with descriptive accounts of events. The approach is not the usual nomothetic exercise of interpreting the events either. It goes beyond the events by interpreting the social processes and unveiling, in the light of theory, the interconnectedness of apparently disunited factors. It represents an involved attempt at exploring the relationship between theory and practice that emphasizes its purposive dimension of social praxis.

Inasmuch as the Marxist theory has normative overtones, the natural question is: how can one overcome ethics in the Marxist hermeneutical activity for ensuring objectivity? This tension between objectivity and ethical subjectivity, when carried to the domain of philosophy, acquires differentiation into scientific materialism and highbrow humanism. Similarly, another question could be: how can one get over the constitutive danger of circularity and tautology involved in the hermeneutical practice of interpreting social processes in theoretically given terms? These limitations exist in alternative hermeneutics as well and none of the alternatives has a way to transcend them. One thing that is certain is that it can never be a Nietzschean kind of positivist and non-philosophical hermeneutics of non-functional history transcending the binary relationship of good and evil.

There are issues around its explanatory apparatus too, whose distinctive focus is on forces of social change that are referred to in different or conflicting metaphorical combinations like 'expressive causality' versus 'material causality'; 'contradictory dynamic' versus 'prime movers'; and so on, besides the limitations of the structural approach such as 'exorbitation of language; attenuation of truth; randomization of history; and capsizal of structures themselves.' In each of these pairs, one expression is relatively more materialistic than the other which is idealistic. Getting rid of the idealist presuppositions has always been a vexed issue in Marxist hermeneutics, which is a totalizing project presupposing philosophical idealism that overshadows historically contingent heterogeneity. The task is to surmount the pull of Kantian, Hegelian idealism, on the one hand, and Gramscian, Lukacsian humanism on the other. It is indeed a question as to how one can interpret history without transcendental Kantianism, teleological Hegelianism, and Lukacsian, Gramscian highbrow humanism. It is also the question of how one interprets history seriously today in the context of post-structuralist deconstruction of solipsistic Cartesianism.

Hermeneutical activity is both theoretical and political in the case of history. It is a political project tied up with a partisan commitment to the future. A historian cannot escape the double bind of both the anticipatory projection and theoretical analysis of the future society. This is forcefully subjective, but at the same time keeping its intellectual procedure open and transparent for methodological evaluation, through which the hermeneutical procedure ultimately turns out to be scientific or objective. The objectivity of a historical interpretation that is avowedly subjective lies in its procedural openness and amenability to empirical verification. Objectivity is not what a historian claims for, but what others attribute to the historical works surviving methodological tests.

Notes

1. Ibn Khaldun, *The Mukhaddhimah: An Introduction to History*, 3 Vols., New York, 1958. See also Ali Al Wardi, *Mantaq Ibn Khaldun*, 2nd Edition, Tunis, 1977.
2. For a recapitulation of the differing assumptions, see Wilhelm Dilthey, *Introduction to Human Sciences*, Translated by Ramon J. Bentanzos, London, 1988, pp. 24-28.
3. See the discussion in Jerome Clubb, "History as a Social Science", *International Social Science Journal*, Vol. XXXIII, No. 4, 1981, pp. 596-609. For a detailed consideration of the inevitable convergence of social sciences and their coming to terms with history, see Abdel Wahab Bouhdiba, "The Social Sciences in Search of Time," ibid., pp. 581-595. There is an extended assessment of the impact of history on social sciences in E.J. Hobsbawm, "Contribution of History to Social Science," ibid., pp. 624-640.
4. See Abdel Wahab Bouhdiba, *Op Cit.*, p. 591.
5. Ibid. Also see E.J. Hobsbawm, *Op Cit.*, pp. 630ff.
6. Barthes, Roland, "Jeunes Chercheurs," in *Le Bruissement de la Langue*. Paris: Le Seuil, 1984. Quoted in Clifford James and George E. Marcus, eds., *Writing Culture*, London, 1986, p.1.
7. Karl Popper, *Conjectures and Refutations*, London, 1963. For arguments specific to the context of history, see his, *Open Society and Its Enemies*, Vol. 2, Rept. 1977, pp. 259-280. It is a test to ensure the scientific nature of history as distinguished from the orthodox ways of doing the subject. For a detailed treatment of the differentiation, see Robert W. Fogel, *Scientific History and Traditional History*, Mass, 1979.

8. Any of the primary readings on the subject provides enough arguments in favor of this. See Marc Bloch, *The Historian's Craft*, Manchester, 1954. E.H. Carr, *What is History*? London, 1963. G. Elton, *The Practice of History*, London, 1970. J. Tosh, *The Pursuit of History*, London, 1984.
9. See the introductory remark in David Harvey, *The Urbanization of Capital*, London, 1985. Preface, p. x.
10. Quoted in K. Jenkins, *Rethinking History*, New York, 1991, p. 47.
11. See Stewart Richards, *Philosophy and Sociology of Science*, London, 1983.
12. Each theory sustains itself within its own meanings, logical measurements and parameters wherein it is never amenable to falsification. See Karl Popper, *Op Cit.*
13. See the discussion on the concept of community of scientists and research traditions in the context of paradigms in Thomas Kuhn, *The Structure of Scientific Revolutions*, Chicago, 1970. Also the concept of sequence of theories ordered into continuous research programmes in I. Lakatos and A. Musgrave, eds., *Criticism and the Growth of Knowledge*, Cambridge, 1970. For a different attitude to the question expressed as 'anything goes,' see P.K. Feyerabend, *Against Method: An Outline of an Anarchistic Theory of Knowledge*, London, 1975.
14. Michel Foucault, *The Archeology of Knowledge*, London, 1972. Also see, Paul Rabinow, *The Foucault Reader*, London, 1984; Alan Sheridan, *Foucault: The Will to Truth*, New York, 1980.
15. Michel Foucault, The Archeology of Knowledge, London, pp. 208-09.
16. Hayden White, *The Tropics of Discourse*, London, 1978. Also see discussions in Keith Jenkins, *Rethinking History*, New York, 1991, p. 71.
17. See the ways in which the theory is defended in G.H. Cohen, *Karl Marx's Theory of History: A Defense*, Princeton, 1978. Also P. Anderson, *In the Tracks of Historical Materialism*, London, 1983; J. Elster, *Making Sense of Marx*, Cambridge, 1985.
18. Karl Marx, *Gundrisse*, Berlin, 1953. See the relevant extracts in E.J. Hobsbawm, ed., *Pre-Capitalist Economic Formations*, London, 1992.

4

Postmodernism and Social Sciences

GURPREET MAHAJAN

What distinguishes postmodernism from most other intellectual discourses is that it goes against received wisdom and challenges the goal of producing universal knowledge and searching for determinate structural identities. Instead of looking for deep meanings and structures in what is the ephemeral present, it denounces meta-narratives and the search for foundations. Paradoxically enough, its own conception of anti-foundationalism is not devoid of its own brand of high theory. It also has an agenda of its own and offers a distinct conception of what is 'social' and how it can be approached and analyzed.

The following pages will be devoted to elaborating and reflecting upon the postmodern theoretical perspective. In particular, the focus will be upon the implications of the perspective for the study of social sciences. For this purpose, the paper will present a composite picture of postmodernism. Instead of separating the different strands within postmodernism, focus will be upon those concepts and philosophical orientations by which we can grasp the particularity of the postmodern way of thinking. The concepts are elucidated by borrowing discriminatingly from the writings of its adherents who belong variously to the pragmatic and post-structuralist traditions in philosophy. Not all the theorists referred to in this presentation describe themselves as postmodern – for instance, Derrida himself did not claim to be postmodern – yet their ideas have been freely used here on the grounds that they share a certain common agenda. Before embarking on our discussion of postmodernism, it is perhaps necessary to reiterate that this paper is not about the thought of any particular philosopher. Hence, it does not reflect upon the changes, shifts or contradictions in an author's position. Instead, it discriminatingly accesses specific texts to illuminate aspects of the intellectual agenda that defines postmodernism.

The Negative Movement

The postmodernist agenda of anti-foundationlism is constituted through two distinct movements: (a) of negation, wherein the search for foundations is criticized, and (b) of affirmation, where its own anti-foundational language is enunciated. The latter, as we shall subsequently notice, is predicated on the former: that is, we can grasp the constitutive elements of the anti-foundational language only after identifying what is foundationalism. Consequently, it is necessary to approach the postmodern agenda through an analysis of its negative movement.

Foundationalism, for the postmodernists, is the search for an absolute and unconditional ground on which existence can be predicated and universal knowledge claims asserted. As such, they maintain that traditional metaphysics and epistemology epitomize foundationalism. The former postulates God as the ultimate ground of all existence, and as a consequence, tries to unveil and discover the presence of this fundamental Being in all beings. It is thus engaged in the determination of Being as presence in all sense of the word. If metaphysics is obsessed with the idea of Being as presence, epistemology too is permeated by the same concern. To this end, it employs the notion of absolute truth and tries to identify the ground on which truth claims can be asserted and arguments conclusively won. Further, it endeavors to determine a universal criterion on the basis of which a vocabulary can be privileged or displaced.

According to the postmodernists, the foundationalist projects of traditional metaphysics and epistemology are shared by philosophy in general. Philosophy, with its emphasis on absolute universals and theory, is quintessentially foundationalist. However, it is not the only form of inquiry that manifests a foundationalist bias. From the postmodernist perspective, science too is a foundational enterprise. Although science questions the notion of an absolute God, the Transcendental is manifested in the scientific secular world in the form of rational plans, or laws of nature and history. Moreover, scientific theories also attempt to present a 'mirror image' of the external world: like philosophy, they claim to discover the truth, or more appropriately, the essential nature of reality. Thus, despite the differences in their respective orientations, postmodernism maintains that both philosophy and science are similar kinds of inquiry as they are committed to the search for foundations or essences of entities. And this search, the postmodernists argue, further entails the uncritical assumption by scientists and philosophers that there exists a super-vocabulary in which the essential and necessary attributes of an entity can be captured and represented.

To put it differently, both philosophy and science postulate the existence of absolute, unified, coherent entities such as nature, history, society and the human self. And both assume that we can recover the essence of these entities without problematizing the nature of linguistic mediation. The only significant difference between them being that philosophy sees reason as the mode of arriving at that identical truth, while science proceeds through systematic observations and generalization. In each case, language is taken to be a self-evident medium of representation, calmly mirroring the world outside.

What unities philosophy and science then, from the perspective of the postmodernists, is the belief that there are non-linguistic things called 'meanings' or 'facts,' and the task of language is to represent them faithfully and accurately. To this end, philosophy frequently assumes a one-to-one relationship between the signifier and the signified, and science presupposes a theory independent, neutral observation language. Both believe that the aim of systematic inquiry is to grasp the essence of an entity, or what amounts to the same thing, its "necessary attributes."[1] The entity in question may be the human self, nature, history, or society; each is said to have an intrinsic nature that the analyst must seek to discover, or more appropriately, uncover.

The alliance between philosophy and science on this account is significant for the postmodernist, because both are paradigmatic human activities, and interestingly enough, they prescribe the same conception of truth, knowledge and science. Both presuppose the existence of essences, and consequently, of universal and unconditional ground. Foundationalism or essentialism is thus their common legacy.

The Enlightenment too was an expression of this legacy as it recommended the search for invariable laws of history[2], and its narratives about the "activities of such entities as the monumental self, or the Absolute Spirit or the Proletariat" were all enterprises inspired by foundationalism.[3] Quite plainly, from the perspective of postmodernism, the Enlightenment and its many projects were deeply flawed. The grand explanatory schemata, or meta-narratives, that sought to describe and predict the movement of such entities as the working class, the rational subject, wealth, spirit or history, suffered from a variety of methodological lacunae: (a) These meta-narratives had been falsified empirically. (b) They imbued each entities with an intrinsic nature, that was there to be discovered by human beings, not made or created by them. Since the intrinsic nature or essence was posited out there, existing quite independent of the agents, these meta-narratives focused on the structure rather than on the agency; they analyzed the laws of historical development, and relatively speaking, neglected the study of consciousness. (c) The meta-narratives of the Enlightenment also obscured the particular in history. In the words of Lyotard, meta-narratives, unlike little stories, do not receive or bestow names. For instance, "the great story of history has its end in the extinction of names (particularisms). At the end of the great story there will simply be humanity. The names 'humanity' has taken will turn out be superfluous, at best they will have designated certain stations along the way to the cross."[4] (d) Meta-narratives tend to reduce the plurality of social processes to the working of a dominant structure or identity. That is, the historical process is analyzed and explained in terms of an identifiable dominant structure. It is seen as the necessary outcome of this primary structure. By arguing that the event is determined by the primary structure, and within Marxism by the primary contradiction, such analyses place a 'closure' upon the historical process and severely constrain freedom.[5]

In sum, foundationalist meta-narratives (including those of the Enlightenment) err in assuming that a particular being has a pre-given, determinate essence. Further, as explanatory schemata, they are reductionist: that is, they explain a particular event by subsuming it under a general law. Informed by the empiricist philosophy of science, these meta-narrative maintain that there is a world 'out there', existing independently of the knower. And the task of philosophical and scientific inquiry is to offer an accurate representation – a mirror image – of that world.

This idea of representation, embodied in the correspondence theory of truth, is challenged by postmodernism. Against the idea of correspondence and accompanying empiricist beliefs, the postmodernists argue the following: (a) We can never know the world as it is in itself. What we have are descriptions (not a representation or mirror image) of the world. These descriptions are presented and communicated linguistically. (b) All descriptions of the world are constructed: that is, we see the world as it appears to us through the limits that are inherent in our language. (c) Since we only have descriptions of the world, we can only speak of these descriptions as being true or false. As such, truth is a property of linguistic entities. It does not refer to an accurate representation of the world in itself. (d) We can no longer speak in terms of an adequate/inadequate vocabulary because language does not seek to provide a mirror image of the reality. Instead, we can examine the way the self is constituted in each vocabulary or language-game. (e) We need to reflect upon the language-game in which sentences are formulated and representations encoded. As the world does not propose a language for us, it does not also tell us what language-game to play. (f) Change from one language-game to another cannot be explained by any one criterion: "...a universal rule of judgment between heterogeneous games is lacking in general"[6]. (g) Since the search for such a universal criterion is rooted in a foundationalist worldview, postmodernist argue that we must resist the temptation to look for a single principle on the basis of which changes in vocabularies can be explained and arguments decisively concluded.

Going Beyond Post-Empiricism

These ideas are, to some extent, familiar. Post-empiricist theories of science had argued along these lines. They had questioned the existence of a neutral observation language and shown that conceptual schemas precede observation. Postmodernism endorsed these views: it accepted that all truth claims – even those embodied in scientific theories – provide plural, diverse and heterogeneous descriptions of the world. However, it supplemented this idea with a critique of all those philosophical systems that endow entities with an essence or intrinsic nature. As such, postmodernism did not offer a statement about the nature of the cognitive process: it made a claim about the nature of being and reality. Seen thus, postmodernism goes far beyond the parameters of the post-empiricist philosophies of science. It rejects both the correspondence theory of truth and the more general search for foundations that it pursued in metaphysics and the Enlightenment meta-narratives. This critique of foundationalism constitutes the negative movement of the postmodern intellectual agenda and represents that which postmodernism is most opposed to. Implicitly, however, these statements about what is conceptually unacceptable also offer a glimpse of the affirmative aspects of the postmodern anti-foundational agenda. They suggest, for instance, that the self, like knowledge claims, is linguistically constituted. Further, truth or the world in itself is inaccessible to us. Hence, it is unprofitable to talk of the nature of truth. What we should speak of instead is self-creation or humanly constituted meanings.

These ideas, when applied to the study of society and history, prompt us to give up the notion of pre-determination, and think, rather, of open-ended and plural historical processes. That is, instead of seeing history as the unfolding of a particular idea – such as progress or liberty – or searching for the underlying laws of temporal succession, we should reflect on the diverse projects that human beings have embarked upon at different moments in time and space. Once again, this idea by itself is not entirely new. Since the end of the eighteenth century, German historians had quartered the ground quite thoroughly on this point. Herder, for instance, had argued that the history of human kind presented a succession of heterogeneous cultures, each complete in itself and possessing its own set of values and cherished goods. The preceding cultures were not, therefore, stepping-stones for the present, and consequently, the values of the present could not be used to judge the earlier forms of cultural lives.[7] Each socio-cultural way of life, according to Herder, had to be understood in its own terms: i.e., in terms of the values internal to it. Subsequently, this methodological insight concerning the historical nature of meanings and truth claims was incorporated in the hermeneutic philosophy of Wilhelm Dilthey.[8]

While hermeneutic philosophy challenged the idea of determination by questioning the belief in a universal historical process, the critics of Marxism emphasized the open-endedness of the historical process. Thus postmodernism was not the first to undertake a critique of the idea of determination. However, what distinguished postmodernism from others in this regard was that it associated determination with the metaphysics of presence. In other words, it did not merely refer to the absence of a pre-determined end or to the presence of plural historical trajectories. Instead, it questioned the belief in determinate, coherent, unified entities and meanings and critiqued all variants of determinism, universality and essence.

The Affirmative Agenda

The simplest way to understand the postmodern anti-foundationalist agenda is to see it as the 'other' of foundationalism. If foundationlism was the language associated with essence, transparency of meaning, representation, determination, and a coherent, unified and single truth, then postmodern anti-foundationalism refers to absent presence, trace, difference, ambiguity, non-determination, plurality, incoherence and inconsistency of meaning. Derrida uses the notion of *arche* writing to elucidate this agenda of anti-foundationalism. He questions the primacy that is generally granted to speech and argues that speech is unable to hold on to the difference between the signifier and the signified. Writing, by comparison, restores the idea of the sign as it resists the reduction of the signifier to the signified. For Derrida, writing is important because it heralds the advent of the exteriority of the signifier.[9]

Just as writing, even in the limited sense of an inscription "carries within it a force of breaking with its contexts, that is, the set of presences which organize the moment of its inscription,"[10] similarly, the sign marks the distance between the signifier and the signified. While Derrida acknowledges that the signifier can signify only if it bears some relation to the signified, yet, from his perspective, the important thing is that the signifier is characterized by a 'surplus': "... it is always the supplement – of the thing itself."[11] It neither exhausts nor is exhausted by the signified. In fact, a graphic sign always "stands for something which is missing, always substitutes itself for the immediate presence of a thing, always shows itself in the stead of the thing itself."[12] Seen thus, the sign is neither a representation nor a copy of the signified, and it cannot also be reduced to a single identifiable meaning or signified. All we can say about the sign, or the text, is that it resonates with many meanings. It is, in other words, multivocal.

Multivocal Texts and Plural Meanings

Multivocality of texts is the basic premise of the postmodern anti-foundational agenda. The idea that texts can have more than one meaning challenges the hermeneutic belief that the text has a pre-given determinate meaning which the original readers can recover as they share with the author a world of inter-subjective meanings and practices.[13] It also questions the accompanying urge to 'fix' the meaning of the text by referring to the intentions of the author or the historical contexts of its origin. In more positive terms, we could say that the notion of multivocality suggests that texts, like any other form of inscription, is autonomous, independent of the author, the original reader, and the context of its origin. It can, and must, therefore be opened to diverse and plural readings.

The point that needs to be emphasized here is that multivocality is the hallmark of all texts: it follows from the nature of sign and is not a consequence of the historical location of the reader. Since there is no pre-determined or *a priori* meaning contained in any text and, what is more important, they lack a coherent, unified meaning, postmodernism asserts that we must play on words and release the multivocality contained in them. To put it in another way, postmodernism argues that reading should not be directed at the recovery of a single, coherent and univocal meaning. Instead, it should focus on the incoherences and ambiguities present in the text. In place of harmonizing the apparent contradictions and bringing out the essential meaning of the text, reading should draw upon the inconsistencies and obscurities inherent in the text and point to the presence of at least two voices within it.

Along with the emphasis on the multivocality of texts, postmodernism emphasizes the absence of determination and fixed pre-given meanings in the text of history; and at another level, it points to the ambiguity and incompleteness of all contexts, social structures, identities and knowledge. Further, it rebels against all forms of conceptual closure and resists the constraints placed upon meanings by historical contexts and authorial intentions. Postmodernism, therefore, allows concepts the freedom to acquire different meanings/signifieds, and views all choices and historical outcomes as being contingent and created. At the epistemological plane, it points out that knowledge is not a system of 'tracking down' or 'discovering' truth.[14] It is, instead, the field of "free play, ... a field of infinite substitutions in the closure of a finite ensemble."[15]

In so far as the free play of the signifier is a mode of introducing the 'other' in the texts, postmodernism's anti-foundational agenda also offers a philosophical perspective in which freedom, diversity and plurality are the core norms. In the context of western capitalist democratic societies, it emphasizes the need to "open the logos of the white man"[16] by creating space for the other within it. As such, it endorses 'new social movements' and lends philosophical support to the struggles of women, gays, greens, blacks, indigenous people, marginalized population etc. Against the Eurocentric perspective of the Enlightenment, it celebrates the ethnic and the oriental. In fact, it makes 'ethnos' an authentic and primary category of social analysis and legitimizes the belief that "groups have a right to speak for themselves and in their own voices."[17] In more general terms, it represents an attitude of tolerance and respect for the other. On the other hand, it assumes that "[i]t is precisely in losing the certainty of truth and the unanimous agreement of others that man becomes an individual",[18] and on the other, it upholds values through which "individuals and communities could co-exist peacefully with other individuals and communities" while also putting together "new syncretic, compromised ways of life."[19]

The postmodernist notion of the freeplay of the signifier also denotes the ideology of self-creation, and in this form it shows that there can be no trans-historical or absolutely valid set of concepts that can provide philosophical foundations for our practical-political choices. These choices have to be made by us, keeping in mind our commitments, aspirations and conceptions of who we are. The belief that political choices and corresponding institutional frameworks are contingent and not based on some "presuppositionless critical reflection" was considered by postmodernists to be a vocabulary better suited for liberal democratic societies. As Rorty explained, in it there is no "trace of divinity...in the form of a divinized world or divinized self."[20] Moreover, it is a vocabulary that gives primacy to 'encounters' and 'conversations' rather than consensus or *homologia.*[21] Conceived in such a manner, the postmodernist project includes a social and political agenda that aims at empowering individuals while simultaneously challenging the existing modes of oppression and domination.

Indeterminacy and Incoherence

Represented thus, postmodernism affirms the idea of plurality, difference, indeterminacy and contingency. As was observed in the preceding section, it endorses all forms of plurality: plural meanings, plural readings/interpretations, plural identities, plural projects of emancipation, plural cultures and plural language-games within a culture. Through the unrestricted pursuit of plurality, postmodernism challenges the notion of a dominant structure, primary identity and deterministic explanatory schemata, while simultaneously supporting the struggles of social and cultural 'others.' Indeed, it facilitates the legitimation of their distant historical and cultural life-worlds and encourages an attitude of tolerance. More than all else, it allows room for the internal 'other.' Instead of pushing it outside the boundaries of national cultural bloc, it accommodates the 'other' within. Seen from this perspective, the postmodernist defense of plurality voices the concerns and the reality of multicultural societies.

As such, in the field of social and cultural life, the ideal of plurality reaffirms the liberal values of tolerance, democracy and equal respect for all. However, its application to the field of knowledge and inquiry creates quite a different scenario. Here, the idea of plural meanings and plural interpretations rules out both the possibility and desirability of seeking universal truths. While the existence of plural meanings negates the possibility of ever arriving at the truth, the active pursuit of the plural and the heterogeneous questions even the desirability of searching for a coherent, unified and universal truth.

Further, the idea of plural meanings engenders a notion of incoherent and ambiguous texts, and incoherent and ambiguous knowledges. To put it differently, in the postmodernist framework, incoherence and ambiguity are aspects associated with plurality and, therefore, inseparable from it. Thus, the presences of plural meanings also indicate the absence of 'fixity' and the lack of a determinate meaning. It calls out to the incompleteness and ambiguity of all readings, thus justifying diverse interpretations of texts. Since no interpretation can, from the postmodernist perspectives, claim to be complete or representative of the truth, there is always room for new and different readings: readings which are located in diverse historical contexts and which draw upon new images and meanings of words. This conception of difference and the associated defense of diversity, even among readings that emanate in the same historical-cultural context, leave the door wide open for epistemological relativism. All readings are now equally valid and no one interpretation can be considered adequate on inadequate. In fact, the postmodernist maintains that questions of adequacy should not be raised because they are formulated in the vocabulary of representation which is itself unacceptable.[22]

What this means effectively is that all readings of texts and all accounts of social reality are equally valid or invalid. Since postmodernists refuse to admit even privilege readings that are aimed at retrieving the author's/agent's intended meaning or readings that seek to contextualize meanings historically, difference and difference alone becomes the guiding norm of all readings. In fact, linked with the strategy of reversing centres and meanings, reading is no longer bound by the author's main concern or central argument in the text. Readers are free to extract, and even isolate, a particular segment of the text and weave their whole interpretation around it, unconstrained by the limitations imposed by other aspects of the text. Since the text is, for the postmodernist, a 'floating signifier'[23] and signs are inherently arbitrary, the reader is granted complete autonomy. The relative autonomy gained by the text through the process of distantiation[24] is now translated as complete freedom to the reader to inscribe and graft new meanings on the texts.

The point that needs to be underlined is that multivocality of texts, in the postmodernist framework, suggests that the signifier is not exhausted by, or limited to, a single, fixed, determinate signified. It can, in other words, have any signified. One cannot, even in a specific context, determine the meaning of a text. Given this sort of indeterminacy and ambiguity of meaning, the text is open to any interpretation, and concepts are vulnerable to diverse appropriations. One can no longer speak of a residual content that can discursively limit the applicability of a particular concept to a given situation.

Three points need to be emphasized here: (a) the particularity and the limitation of the postmodernist anti-foundational agenda is that it associates plurality with indeterminacy, incoherence, ambiguity, and most of all, equivocality; (b) plurality of readings is, in their framework, not an expression of the limitations placed on knowledge; it is instead a desired epistemological ideal. The idea of play/indeterminacy of the sign makes a virtue of different reading and, with it, of epistemological relativism; (c) previously, the theorists spoke of the improbability of predicting with certainty what might happen. They provided space for human intervention and effect-variation. However, in doing so, they did not doubt the existence of a structured pattern of interaction among these diverse variables, nor did they doubt the ability of a particular structure to generate a specific effect. What was challenged was the conclusion that the existence and preponderance of a particular structure would necessarily produce a given, pre-determined effect. Postmodernism, on the other hand, questions the assumption underlying this way of thinking. Through its conception of ambiguous and "undecidable" structures and "unstable relationships,"[25] it, in effect, rejects, *tout court*, the idea of a structure and of patterned regularities

The notion of incoherent and ambiguous structures also rule out explanations, however incomplete, partial or limited they might be. If structures are incoherent and their relationship with other structures irregular and ambiguous, then we cannot even theoretically associate an effect with a particular structure. Hence, even *post-hoc* retrospective explanations become inconceivable in this rendering of the anti-foundational agenda. As such, all attempts to identify a coherent structure or its necessary attributes and determinate relationships are suspect within postmodernism; in fact they are avoided because they are also aimed at 'fixing' or determining meaning. In so far as explanations require that we theoretically and temporarily close-off what in reality is an 'open' system, there is no room for them in the postmodern agenda. Postmodernism is opposed to the introduction of every kind of closure, even a methodologically postulated temporary closure. Consequently, indeterminacy that was, for the critics of historical determinism, an attribute of ontological existence, now becomes a feature of epistemological enquiry.

Thus, postmodernism distinguishes itself from all these forms of anti-foundationalism by questioning both ontological and epistemological foundationalism. Further, by associating difference and plurality with indeterminacy and ambiguity, it undermines both explanation and systematic inquiry. Its critique of unified entities questions not only the notion of a unified society and a systematic whole, but also that of a unified subject/process/event, possessing a determinate form and identity. In addition, postmodernism views as suspect all attempts to transcend the particular and the ephemeral. The desire to pin down something that does not merely apply to one person once is thus completely damned.[26] In its place, particularity, or more accurately, singularity is cherished and characterized as being the 'other' of foundationalist philosophy. The obsession with uniqueness and singularity delegitimizes the search for generalizations and severely constrains the subject by trapping it in the momentary and the ephemeral. The subject, focusing on the 'here' and 'now', and forgetful of its own history, can, however, hardly be expected to distance herself from her inherited conceptions.

Viewed in this way, the postmodernist anti-foundationalism postulates a conception of self and society that raises serious problems. The postmodern defense of indeterminacy and incoherence makes schizophrenia the norm of everyday life, and its denial of narrative continuity and understanding jeopardizes both social life and social interaction. In fact, it places the social and the societal under erasure. "The social," it suggests, "only exists in the vain attempt to institute that impossible object: society."[27] In the absence of the social, what remains is an aggregate of "centreless" individuals or "random assemblages of contingent and idiosyncratic needs."[28]

Derrida's delegitimation of the study of 'origins' and historically contextualized analyses of meanings is thus supplemented by a denial of the social and an interrogation of both structure and system. This, together with the mistrust of meta-narratives, allows the postmodernist to legitimize the study of the particular in itself. The study of the event as an evanescent "one off-happening"[29] without any history or follow up, structural or systemic constraints, becomes the order of the day. Given the disillusionment with Marxism, postmodernism encourages cultural studies that freely examine any and every cultural practice irrespective of its place in the system of signification that characterize a given society and social order. It also sanctions readings of these cultural practices in a vocabulary that is borrowed neither from the agent nor from that of the community. In other words, it allows complete freedom to the reader to construct the practice in an imaginative, bold and different way. The ability of the reader to place new images is now cherished more than any reflection of a determinate meaning. Boldness of conjectures and readings thus characterize the postmodern enquiry.

Conclusion

The value of postmodern enquiry resides primarily in its critique of those meta-narratives that are woven around a dominant structure and a primary identity. Its reference to the internal 'other' points, quite perceptively, to the limitations of the meta-narratives of the Enlightenment. However, its own anti-foundational agenda, postulated in terms of endless plurality, indeterminacy, incoherence and contingency, generates norms that vitiate social existence, communication, understanding and explanation. Although some of its adherents employ the idea of indeterminacy to argue that "everything is in human hands"[30] and, in this sense create, not discover, the absence proof. Any discussion of structural constraints reduces contingency to the play of chance. Eventually, its theoretical stance vitiates consistent action and struggle. The postmodernist agents, aware of the incoherence and ambiguity of all structures, projects and life-worlds, can hardly be expected to commit themselves to political struggles, which invariably seek to fix meaning. Political struggle and action is further made difficult by the postmodernist belief that at the end of the dialogue is 'paralogy' i.e., "paradoxes, discontinuities and undecidabilities of utterances".[31] Since, dissension rather than consensus is the motivational, force in encounters, and even "consensus obtained through discussion" is seen as doing "violence to the heterogeneity of language-games"[32], and by extension, to our freedom. There is no real possibility of achieving an agreement that can bind agents engaged in political struggle.

Given these analytical difficulties, we need to distinguish the negative movement from the affirmative agenda of postmodernism. As a critique of metaphysics of presence and theories of correspondence, postmodernism provides perceptive insights; but the concepts through which it delineates its anti-foundationalism are beset with a variety of theoretical difficulties. In particular, the association of anti-foundationalism with the presence of ambiguity, incoherence and relentless difference dissolves the textual object itself. As such, it undermines both societal existence and systematic scientific inquiry. On the one hand, it excludes the possibility of offering even the partial explanations, and on the other, it jeopardizes communication and understanding in the social world.

Notes

1. Laclau, E., *New Reflections on the Revolution of Our Time*, London: Verso, 1990, p. 144.
2. See Buckle, H.T., *Civilization in England*, Vol. 1, London: Watts & Co, 1930. Also, Bury, J.B., "The Science of History," in F. Stern (ed.), *The Varieties of History: From Voltaire to the Present*, London: Thames & Hudson, 1970.

3. Rorty, R., *Philosophy and the Mirror of Nature*, Oxford: Basil Blackwell, 1980, p.585. See also Lyotard, J.F., *The Postmodern Condition: A Report on Knowledge*, Translated by G. Bennington and B. Massumi, Manchester: Manchester University Press, 1987, p. xxiii.
4. Lyotard, J.F., *The Different: Phrases in Dispute*, Translated by G. van Deer Abbele, Minneapolis: University of Minnesota Press, 1988, p. 155.
5. Laclau, *Op cit.*, p. 50.
6. Lyotard, *The Different*, p. xi.
7. See Herder, J.G., *On Social and Political Structure*, Translated and edited by F.M. Barnard, Cambridge: Cambridge University Press, pp. 188-231.
8. See Mahajan, Gurpreet, *Explanation and Understanding in Human Sciences*, New Delhi: Oxford University Press, 1992, pp. 50-58.
9. Derrida, J., *Of Grammatology*, Translated by Gayatri C. Spivak, Baltimore, Maryland: John Hopkins University Press, 1976, p. 14.
10. Derrida, J., *Margins of Philosophy*, Translated by Alan Bass, Chicago: University of Chicago Press, 1982, p. 317.
11. Derrida, *Of Grammatology*, p. 145.
12. Bannet, E.T., *Structuralism and the Logic of Dissent*, London: Metheun, 1989, p. 191.
13. Mahajan, *Op cit.*, pp. 52-57.
14. See Rorty, R., "The Contingency of Language," *London Review of Books*, 1986, 17 April. Also, Rorty, R., "The Contingency of Selfhood," *London Review of Books*, 1986, 8 May.
15. Derrida, *Of Grammatology*, p. 51.
16. Bannet, *Op cit.*, p. 223.
17. Harvey, D., *The Condition of Postmodernity*, Oxford: Basil Blackwell, 1989, p. 48.
18. Rorty, R., "Philosophers, Novelists and Inter-Cultural Comparisons: Heidegger, Kundera and Dickens," Conference Paper, Honalulu, July 31-August 11, 1989.

19. Rorty, R., "A Pragmatist View of Rationality and Cultural Difference," Paper Presented in Delhi, 26 December, 1990.
20. Rorty, R., "The Contingency of Community," *London Review of Books,* 1986, 24 July.
21. Lyotard, *The Postmodern Condition,* p. 28.
22. Rorty, "The Contingency of Language", *Op cit.*
23. Laclau, *Op cit.*, p. 28.
24. Ricoeur, P., *Hermeneutics and the Human Sciences,* Cambridge: Cambridge University Press, 1981, pp. 137-43.
25. Laclau, *Op cit.*, p. 30.
26. Rorty, R., "The Contingency of Selfhood", *Op cit.*
27. Laclau, *Op cit.*, p. 92.
28. Rorty quoted in O'Sullivan, N., "Political Integration, the Limited State, and the Philosophy of Postmodernism," *Political Studies,* XLI, 1993, 21-42.
29. Baumann, Z., "Survival as a Social Construct," in M. Featherstone (ed.), *Cultural Theory and Cultural Change,* London, Sage, 1992, p. 30.
30. ibid.
31. Holub, R.C., *Jurgen Habermas: Critic in the Public Sphere,* London: Routledge, 1991, p. 142.
32. Lyotard, *The Postmodern Condition,* p. xxv.

5

The Limits of the Objectivity Paradigm

T.V.S. RAMAMOHAN RAO

'Objectivity', viewed as a property of impartial, logical and of scientific propositions, can have but a limited scope. It cannot guarantee that a logically deduced proposition is a unique explanation of a universal fact. Similarly, when there are persistent differences in behavior, it may not be possible to generate a single objective explanation. It is also difficult to conceptualize an objective basis for choosing from the alternative explanations. A flexible interpretation of objectivity would be called for if the differences among the individual units of observation are more important than their common features.

1. The Issues

The need for a scientific inquiry arises only if the following three axioms are acknowledged:

(a) There is a fundamental interaction between (i) the human beings, (ii) the animal world, and (iii) nature (inanimate things),

(b) Human beings, and to a limited extent even animals, make attempts to utilize these interactions to enhance their welfare, and

(c) Economizing on human effort necessitates accumulation of knowledge in a systematic fashion so that it can be retrieved as and when needed instead of 'reinventing the wheel.' For, experience suggests that useful information is expensive and time consuming.

Viewed against this backdrop, it can be argued that the perspective on science depends upon what use it will be put to.

Ancient societies believed in living in harmony with nature. Consequently, they made attempts to (a) understand the rhythms of nature, and (b) specify the goals of life that are in consonance with the limitations set by nature. To achieve their goals, they needed (a) a knowledge of the phenomena that can be predicted with some certainty, (b) an organized way of recording facts, and (c) a classification system that facilitates efficient retrieval. The immensity of the task and the limitations of human intellect necessitated such a structured approach to science.

Note that they also recognized the necessity to modify the otherwise cooperative nature to improve their well-being. The invention of fire to cook food and keep warm, the identification of shelter from the elements, and the wheel come to mind at once. To an extent these artifacts (a) have been suggested by the analogies in nature itself, (b) tend to utilize natural laws to achieve the goals, and (c) do not in anyway go against the natural laws. Given these impressive features of ancient peoples' living condition, the achievements of ancient civilizations were certainly very scientific. On the other hand, modern societies (especially the western countries) (a) faced hostile climates that necessitated major modifications of the natural rhythms, and (b) found the necessity to augment the supply of commodities provided by nature in its normal cycles.

As a result, Western societies made attempts to (a) define the needs and aspirations of individuals in the society, and (b) examine the ways and means of taming nature to suit human needs. Some of these activities were such that they did not unduly disturb the natural balances ingrained in the ecosystem. Such an application of certain physical, chemical, and/or biological principles and the alterations proved beneficial in producing more and better commodities as in the case of natural fertilizers, hot houses to produce vegetables and flowers, and so on.

However, when some improperly understood phenomena were encountered and/or some aspects of scientific evidence were neglected, there were disasters due to nature's fury, as evident from (i) historical events like the plague that wiped out half the population of London, and (ii) the more recent phenomena like the ecological crisis, the spread of AIDS, and so on. In other words, a proper and objective understanding of phenomena has been essential for the functioning of modern societies. Primarily for this reason, modern science tends to emphasize (a) understanding certain basic facts of nature, (b) stating the goals to be achieved, (c) detailing the problems to be tackled, and (d) developing an efficient solution to the problem.

For the purposes of conducting scientific inquiry, natural phenomena can be classified into one of the three types: (a) Some of them are universal. The fact of gravitation is one such example. (b) Some phenomena have a great deal of fixity though there are some differences among individual units. For example, the water available at most places has significant common properties, though there are differences from one place to another. (c) The differences among individual units are sometimes much prominent compared to the commonalties. The different varieties of soil and their ability to sustain different types of vegetation is a case in point. The analyst must first decide which of these aspects – the commonalities or the differences – need emphasis.

These distinctions are important even in the context of generating a solution to practical problems. (1) Suppose there is universality of the phenomenon. Then, one common solution would be sufficient. For instance, a well-defined and universally applicable solution can tell us when the next total solar eclipse will occur in India. (2) Following general principles would be helpful in most cases. Suppose we go into the kitchen to fix a meal. Definitely, it should be possible to draw upon some recipe that is known to produce a palatable meal if the instructions are followed closely. However, the final product will be somewhat different based on some amount of judgment, individual tastes, and the available ingredients. (3) However, when approaching problems associated with individuals, such as psychiatric issues, the differences between the patients are more fundamental compared to the common features that they exhibit. In such cases, as Feyerabend puts it, acknowledging the differences is the essence of objectivity even if we cannot explain them.[1]

The argument that the common features are predominant defined the nature of science that developed over the years. In other words, science was sought to be made universal by neglecting the major differences even when they occur in nature. At best some classification systems were adopted to make the distinctions. Stated in this format, it is obvious that there are two clearly distinguishable dimensions of scientific research, viz., (a) the choice of substantial issues (some tend to argue that they should also be of practical relevance and not just scientific curiosity), and (b) the method of extracting scientific information and validation.

Quite clearly, the criteria of objectivity will be different in these two cases. However, it is somewhat unfortunate that a satisfactory methodological approach to the first is not attempted. Instead, the scientific method generally emphasizes the logical form of deductive reasoning as applied to (b) above. The objectivity paradigm is therefore severely limited in its scope.

Within the limited boundaries of objectivity considerations, the essential issues for methodological considerations are: (a) what constitutes acceptable knowledge or information?, (b) how can we go about building it?, (c) should deviations from conventions and the development of innovative new theories be allowed even if they still do not have the 'acceptable' logical form?, and (d) is it worthwhile to utilize information or hypotheses that are not fully scientifically demonstrated even if the solution to a practical problem demands it?

The rest of the paper is organized as follows. Section 2 deals with the dimensions of objectivity in scientific procedures. Objectivity of facts is the theme of section 3. Section 4 considers in detail the types of theories and the implications of the objectivity paradigm. Some further thoughts, that deserve more elaborate consideration, will be outlined in section 5.

2. Dimensions of Objectivity

The use of the word 'objectivity' has already entered the argument unwittingly. It is necessary to attend to its definition in more specific terms. It is worthwhile reminding ourselves that the present state of knowledge does not distinguish between the criteria necessary for the analysis of the choice of issues that deserve emphasis, and the method of generating the knowledge. As the Oxford Dictionary puts it, objectivity involves an impartial judgment and the ability to free oneself from personal prejudice. In any scientific discourse this criterion must be applied to both (a) the collection of facts or the specification of the phenomenon that needs to be explained, and (b) the principles that relate several facts in the scientist's effort to understand nature.

A somewhat more specific description of objectivity is perhaps possible. Consider a collection of facts. It may be postulated that a fact is objectively stated if and only if (a) its validity can be established by observation, and (b) it is stated in the same way by everyone concerned with it. It is necessary to have universal conventions and labels to catalogue such facts. Now consider the following statements: (i) the rose is red, and (ii) the leaf is green. Here the rose and the leaf are identified by convention. The case of the specification of red and green is similar. However, the Shakespearian adage that "a rose will smell as sweet even if we call it by any other name" suggests that it would be futile to look for objectivity in the choice of conventions. The best that can be expected is that the scientists involved in the endeavor should not violate the agreed upon conventions. This way of approaching the specification of objectivity assumes that any fact and every fact that the scientist wants to examine constitute worthwhile knowledge. No judgment is entertained.

Similarly, a theory or scientific explanation of a phenomenon entails relating certain facts with others according to the following:

$F_1 \rightarrow R \rightarrow F_2$

Where F_1 is one subset of facts,

R is a set of concepts and relationships, and

F_2 is another subset of facts.

See, for instance, the work of Margenau.[2] For such a theory to be objective, it is necessary to have (a) a well-defined catalogue of concepts, (b) a method of relating facts and concepts, and (c) a possibility of replication irrespective of who the analyst is. However, the unidirectional flow, as stated above, is not quite valid as a representation of theory. It is necessary to acknowledge other valid alternatives, such as two-way causation, as well.

It may appear that the requirement of objectivity as stated above would also make the facts and theories universal. However, a scientific principle to be valid can be considered to be a universal truth if and only if it is (a) objectively deduced, and (b) it is valid for all time and place. These two are perhaps closely related in the physical and biological sciences. For example, the scientific calculation regarding the total solar eclipse on October 24, 1995 was valid up to the last second at places that were identified ahead of time. However, there are exceptions even in the context of such sciences. For instance, witness the enormous differences among the physical features of human beings of the same sex and a given species of animals. Fundamentally, the task of scientifically explaining all the minute details of the differences may never be possible. As a result, differences persist and (a) an explanation may not be in sight as yet, or (b) more than one theory, satisfying the conditions of objectivity, may persist. In sum, it can be argued that the requirement of universality *per se* is redundant. What is needed, however, is transparency of the argument and its replicability under stated conditions. Objectivity should mean this and perhaps only this.

One further issue should be highlighted. There cannot be any objective procedure for choosing (a) which facts to study and which to ignore, and (b) which method of analysis is more objective than another. In most practical situations, we may be in the position of a proverbial drunkard who is searching under the lamp-post for the keys he lost because there is more light there.

Only the following three aspects of the objectivity paradigm will be considered in the rest of the paper:

(a) Is the theory or argument logically consistent?,

(b) Can its validity be established by observation?, and

(c) Is it stated in the same way by everyone concerned with it? It will be argued that

 (i) the degree of difficulty in ensuring objectivity increases as we move from (a) to (b) to (c) stated above, and

 (ii) the requirements of objectivity cannot be the same while dealing with different aspects of science.

In sum, the objectivity paradigm

(a) refers to the form of scientific discourse,

(b) applies the same standards to the same substance of scientific investigation, and

(c) is too rigid in its insistence that only one of the many plausible (and logically consistent) explanations is the truth. However, the criteria for ascertaining objectivity do not clearly specify a method of choosing the valid explanation.

3. Objectivity in the Choice of Facts

Recall that a fact can be taken to be objectively stated if and only if (a) its validity can be established by observation, and (b) it is stated in the same way by everyone concerned with it. It is possible to argue that this is too hard a requirement. Situation can be conceptualized where (i). the fulfillment of either of the condition may have to be accepted, or (ii) neither is necessary for the existence of a fact.

Fundamentally, facts derive their existence from the possibility of human perception and giving expression through the use of some language. Consider the following statement:

There is a finite amount of time between successive appearances of the sun in the east at any specified geographical location though there are rhythmic variations over longer periods of time.

In stating this, I have already assumed that 'the sun' and 'the east' are concepts agreed upon by convention. However, certain 'facts' may not come to light because people fail to acknowledge them. For example, a blind man may not appreciate ideas like 'the sunrise' and 'the east'. The statement, however, is still a fact.

This problem is found persisting in both physical and the social sciences. For instance, consider the magnetic or electrical properties of certain materials. These properties should have been in existence in reality even before they were discovered and/or formalized as facts. Similarly, consider the complaints regarding the gender bias in social interaction. We cannot say that this is not a fact (or a social problem that has been around) simply because some of us have not been able to articulate the dimensions of the problem and/or make others acknowledge it. Condition (a) above is not necessary for the existence of facts. Now consider property (b). Examine the following statement:

I saw a large pinkish object in the sky yesterday night.

I do not see why it cannot be a fact even if nobody else noticed it and the object may not appear again. But within the parameters of practice, the scientific conventions would not allow it.

However, there is no consistent application of this practice. For, historical observations, which face a similar problem, have to come to pass. Consider, for example, the following statement:

The Jews crucified Jesus Christ.

None of us observed the event, and the possibility of replication does not arise. The issue is: in our quest for objective facts, whose observation shall we trust and whose observation shall we reject? I will leave this as a rhetorical question. But the essence of the argument is that even property (b) is not necessary to determine the objectivity of a fact. It is fairly simple to see that criteria (a) and (b) are not sufficient conditions either. The following illustration is revealing. Suppose a thousand different people call a cow a donkey. Is it in fact a donkey then? This is not possible if everyone understands and truthfully follows the labeling and conventions defined by science.

Another aspect that is always contestable is the division of facts between F_1 and F_2. there is no objective way of saying that certain facts are primitive and belong to F_1 and others need an explanation and are therefore to be classified as F_2. Consider the following:

A full solar eclipse occurred at 8.21 AM on October 24, 1995.

All of us observed it. Shall we call it an element of F_1? Or is it more reasonable to take the position that it needs an explanation and put it into F_2? Once again, I leave these as rhetorical questions. Considerations of objectivity do not appear to have yet reached this realm of discourse.

Let me conclude this part of the argument thus: Neither has there been any attempt nor does it seem possible if we want to identify a logical formalism to identify objective facts. The identification and specification of facts will remain specific to culture and time.

4. Objective Relationships (Theories)

Following the conventions set up by Margenau, alluded to in section 2, it is possible to conceptualize four types of relationships. In general, a relationship establishes a link between

(a) a fact in F_1 and a fact in F_2,

(b) elements of F_1 and a theoretical construct,

(c) a theoretical construct and an element of F_2, or

(d) two constructs.

To begin with, note that a construct is a logical formalism defined by the theorist to provide a method of setting up an association. We generally find two types of constructs.

(a) Some constructs are amenable to verification by a controlled experiment. One example of this nature is the resultant of two forces.

(b) Other concepts do not allow such direct verification. The following examples are typical:

 (i) binary arithmetic, and (ii) national income.

These concepts are such that no amount of searching for facts through primary observation would ever disclose them. They are devices set up by the analyst to facilitate logical formalism.

In the context of the first group of concepts it is possible to adhere to the objectivity criteria, since (a) they can be verified by direct observation, and (b) there is an invariance with respect to the observer, and perhaps, over time and space as well. The other subsets of constructs are more troublesome if we insist on the same kind of objectivity. Consider the case of arithmetic. All of us endorse that

(a) $1 + 1 = 2$

(b) $2 - 1 = 1$, and

(c) $5 > 2$

These logical conventions were set up by the mathematician to facilitate consistency (objectivity?) in the use of numbers arithmetic. There is a general agreement that such a logic is essential to avoid confusion. However, there is nothing unique or objective about this logic. For,

(a) we can equally replace it by some other procedure like the binary logic. In this convention $1 + 1 = 1\emptyset$, and an internally consistent arithmetic has been developed on this basis.

(b) In social interaction, we acknowledge synergies. Consider the following example: *Neither Krishna nor Sarthi, acting in isolation, will be able to lift a refrigerator from a truck. However, the two together can.* Basically a logic like $1 + 1 > 2$ has emerged and internally consistent arithmetic operations have been defined.

Three aspects of such constructs should be highlighted:

(a) there is no such thing as an objective method for choosing constructs,

(b) an objective way of validating constructs and theories by empirical observation is as yet elusive, and

(c) in several instances, there is a tendency to re-classify constructs as facts if they are used often enough and found to be satisfactory for the purpose of which they are defined.

Secondly, the choice of certain constructs is purely subjective even in the physical sciences and mathematics. The logic of the quantum theory in contrast to that of the wave theory is a case in point. In the realm of social sciences, institutional arrangements such as marriage, and the market, are set up by the analysts for a specific purpose and there is no uniqueness in these institutions even for the stated purpose. It is possible to visualize alternative institutional arrangements that serve the purpose just as well. It is almost always impossible to say what constitutes an objective choice of constructs.

With these limitations in perspective, we may now consider each of the four relationships alluded to earlier.

(a) F to F

The following statement is a typical example in this group:

The atmospheric temperature has gone down because the sun has set.

It is basically an 'if-then' statement. It is the use of 'because' that signals its classification as a relationship. Now consider the argument that *the sun has set* is neither necessary nor sufficient for the occurrence of the event, viz., that the atmospheric temperature has gone down. There are at least some conditions (however idealized they may appear) under which this relationship is false, e.g., the atmospheric pressure will be low even when the sun is bright if there is a great deal of snow on the ground and/or it is windy. On the other hand, the drop in the temperature after the sun has set will not be appreciable if we are close to the ocean. To claim universality or objectivity, it is necessary to specify all the conditions under which a fact in F can materialize. Such a search is almost futile.

Let us now consider the second relationship.

(b) F to R

Economic analysis often postulates relationships between elements of F_1 and some constructs or concepts that do not have an empirical counterpart. Consider the statement:

An increase in the statutory liquidity ration (SLR) imposed by the Reserve Bank of India (RBI) reduces the money supply in the economy.

In this case, the concept of 'money supply' is something created for analytical convenience and reveals itself only when a specific procedure, for combining elements of F_1, is adopted for its computation. Two aspects are noteworthy here:

(i) Is there anything objective about the measurement of money supply? In economic analysis this concept is not an end (or a goal) in itself. It is functional, and is used in explaining some other phenomenon. It was shown that the usefulness of the definition (M_1, M_2, M_3) depends on the ultimate purpose. The constructs are generally 'valid' only because we say so, and *not* because they can be verified by observation.

(ii) Even if we accept the definition, we only have a sufficient condition. This gives rise to the possibility that an equally valid explanation for the decrease in money supply may be offered. There is as yet no 'objective' way of distinguishing between two logically consistent theories.

However, from the viewpoint of formal logic, the statement cannot be refuted even if we accept the concept and the premises. That is, there can be objectivity about the logical consistency of each of the theories, but no objectivity about which one is correct.

(c) R to F

Attempts to explain certain facts in F_2 often provoke the analyst to build concepts on the basis of which relationships can be set up. Consider the following examples:

Ex 1: *An increase in the permanent income of the individual increases the demand for durable consumer goods.*

Ex 2: *The rigidities in organizational responses often result in the failure of firms.*

While considering such theories we should be clear about

(i) what we mean by 'permanent income' and 'rigidities...,' and

(ii) what the logical process of deduction is.

Once these requirements are met, objectivity can be claimed in the sense that the requirement of formal logic are satisfied. There is nothing unique about such theories.

(d) R to R

A great deal of theory in social sciences deals with the relationships between two or more concepts. Consider the well-known Keynesian macroeconomic theory. It has relationships like

C = aggregate consumption = cY

Y= national income, and

I_a= autonomous investment.

Then, as an identity

$$Y = C + I_a$$

Hence,

$$Y = I_a / (1-c)$$

Note that the concepts like C and Y reveal themselves only when we define them, and specify a measurement procedure. Once this procedure is accepted the last expression is always correct. The analysis is objective only in that sense. It is well known that there are at least two other logically consistent approaches to the explanation of Y:

(i) the Classical theory, and

(ii) the Rational Expectations approach.

Each of these provides a sufficient condition. There is no objective way of choosing between them.

Some theories, while they appear plausible *a priori*, may not satisfy the strict requirements of logic.

Ex 1: *An increase in income inequality in the society has led to an increase in the incidence of crime.*

Ex 2: *The hasty implementation of the liberalization programme resulted in an evaluation of the common stock of the public undertakings.*

The fundamental problem in such cases is in arriving at acceptable (let alone objective) definitions of 'crime' and 'the correct valuation of the common stock.' Even the logic through which the relationships are sought to be established is not always clear. Definitely, there is a need to impose strict logical standards on those who enunciate such theories.

The requirement of verifiability through observation and replication (even if it is only under ideal conditions) are much more difficult in the context of such theories. What the social sciences sought to do was to

(i) establish a measurement procedure, and

(ii) utilize some clearly defined statistical procedures for verification.

Objectivity was supposed to mean rule-following, e.g., following through the logical statistical procedures. However, the justification for why these procedures should be accepted is not always clear. Even if we do not question this, the techniques

(i) cannot categorically establish the validity of most theories of this nature, and
(ii) introduce biases whose magnitude cannot be ascertained by any objective procedure.

Let me hasten to add that these are my judgments based on experience rather than a matter of universal acknowledgement.

Social phenomena, taken in their totality, are extremely complex. As Arrow puts it, "until [recently] the choice open to a theorist was between a vague analysis which covered all factors and a precise analysis of an over-simplified model, and it is not surprising that the former was frequently found useful for purposes of overall economic analysis."[3] There are many details of the observed phenomena that defy logical explanation. This is the primary reason for the inability to incorporate them into logically consistent models. However, the normative aspect of social science, which emphasizes the need for an immediate solution to a current problem, cannot wait indefinitely for the ultimate truth before devising a solution.

This section can be concluded with the following observations:

(a) Objectivity is the essence of the procedure for accumulating knowledge, or what Simon labels as procedural rationality.[4]
(b) There is no denying the fact that there is a need for some logically consistent reasoning. This is the minimal level of objectivity that can be enforced.
(c) Once this condition is satisfied, it would be best to allow the rich variety of theories or explanations that are possible. Trying to set out logical procedures to choose one out of

them as the only valid theory is neither meaningful nor desirable from a substantive viewpoint. Dogmatic insistence on uniqueness would be counter-productive.

5. A Pretense at a Conclusion

Transparency is the hallmark of all logical procedures. This is desirable from the viewpoint of all scientific discourses in so far as the user can be confident that it can be replicated. The minimal standards of objectivity should therefore be

(a) to state the assumptions or facts being used as premises,

(b) to detail the logical method of deduction, and

(c) to state all the conclusions in a verifiable form (from a logical viewpoint, if not an empirical perspective)

However, it was observed that enterprising alternative theorizing or ideas are put forward on some occasions. In almost all such instances, going off the beaten track revolutionized scientific thinking. The theory of relativity is a case in point. The Keynesian macroeconomics that turned the classical argument upside down is also of similar vintage. This suggests that stifling creativity in the name of logical objectivity is not desirable. It would be necessary to pay attention to the substance of analysis and discourse. Stated somewhat differently, a rich variety of theories, each one of which satisfies the conditions of logical coherence, will be needed to explain scientific phenomena. Science would be richer, if this variety can be generated, instead of a sterile insistence on universality.

There are also situations, like what is often described as science fiction, where the analyst is allowing his imagination to get better of the logical formalism. However, on further scientific exploration some of them proved possible. The case of satellites to the moon illustrates this very well. Though lacking in rigour initially, such theories could eventually be brought under the scientific ambit. From the viewpoint of substantive rationality, it may be desirable to allow such flights of fancy rather than reject them as not being objective. I will not give priority, let alone pride of place, to the logical form and requirements of objectivity, though I consider them necessary evil. Because going against them can lead to disastrous consequences.

In an ultimate sense, it must be acknowledged that individuals have different

(a) capacities to comprehend changes,

(b) reactions to a given stimulus,

(c) capacities to adjust to changes, and

(d) objectives in their daily encounter with science.

The scientific approach must ultimately cater to all these nuances. The current practice has been to concentrate on commonalities and to look for and advocate universal solutions. However, in more recent times logically consistent analytical procedures are becoming available to study the differences in the behavior patterns. For example, in economic analysis the rational expectations approach was successful in showing that there is a logical way of arguing that the unexpected and/or dissimilar properties are the more important sources of the differences in the behavior of certain economic variables. In a similar vein, the realities of cyberspace and internet promise the possibility of dealing with each individual as a different entity and provide means to satisfy specific objectives. This is currently a reality in a very limited sphere like providing information or entertainment. But the potential to spread the net wide and cover many other aspects of human existence appears to be possible. Some progress is therefore in sight, but it is as yet premature to attempt any generalization.

In the very near future, objectivity in scientific research may indeed mean the ability to understand individual idiosyncrasies and utilizing the differences in the behavioral patterns to set up specialized solutions without having to sacrifice the requirements of formal logic. The issues involved here are of practical importance and should therefore receive more attention.

Notes

1. Feyerabend, P.K., "Knowledge and the Role of Theories," *Philosophy of Social Science*, 18 (1988), 157-178.
2. Margenau, H., "What is a Theory?", in S.R. Krupp (ed.), *The Structure of Economic Science*, Englewood Cliffs: Prentice Hall, 1966.
3. Arrow, K.J. "Historical Background," in K.J. Arrow, S. Karlin, and H. Scarf (eds.), *Studies in the Mathematical Theory of Inventory and Production*, Stanford, 1958.
4. Simon, H.A., "Rationality as Process and as Product of Thought", *American Economic Review*, 68 (1978), 1-16.

6

Social Reality and Social Theory

BIJOY H. BORUAH

A scientific enquiry is, roughly and broadly speaking, directed at *finding out the truth about something,* something of the real world, through a proper analysis and explanation of facts and phenomena. A *natural* scientific enquiry aims at finding out the nature of physical reality, the natural universe of matter and motion in all its complexity. It is a search for a true account of the *structure* and *function* of natural phenomena in its endless variety. On the basis of observation and experiments, hypothesis and theories are built and these are in turn tested by further experiments, and then laws are established which embody general truths about respective phenomena or segments of nature. On the basis of these well-established and invariant laws, the enquirer facilitates herself to the prediction and control of nature through appropriate technological inventions.

Physical reality is not everything that we inquire about. The human mind has always been deeply concerned with human existence itself – that is, human social existence rather than biological existence. There is, therefore, *human reality* for us to find out the truth about. Human reality is not obviously reducible to physical reality, and hence it deserves an approach that is appropriate to its essential characteristics. In a way, one can say that there are human facts to be explained or understood in a distinctive manner – these human facts or phenomena being characteristically contrasted with physical facts or natural phenomena. Human social reality has its own kind of complexity and variety, demanding analysis and interpretation of its own kind.

The question therefore is whether our enquiry into the nature of human social phenomena can also be designated as a *scientific* study. In a way this question is already answered by the existence of what is known as 'social sciences' over more than a century. Various facets of human social existence are studied by the various social sciences such as sociology, psychology, anthropology, politics, economics, law, and so on. Some of these sciences are strongly modelled on the natural sciences in that they use the techniques of quantification, statistics, controlled experimentation, testing of hypothesis and other devices and principles. But others are quite different in character. From this it should be obvious that there is not enough methodological unity amongst the social sciences.

Whether a particular social science is methodologically closer to natural sciences or characteristically distinct from the latter, there is a general fact that lies at the heart of any social science. And this general fact is that the social sciences all concern themselves with the human, mentally endowed, acting members of the world, members or individuals that are fundamentally unlike in nature from the inanimate objects of reality. The human society is constituted of such mentally endowed, self-conscious agents in their interrelations. Social reality is therefore the reality of human thoughts and emotions and actions all woven into a complex and variegated fabric of human social existence.

Social reality, or the human world, is unlike the non-human world of physical reality in that it is a reality constituted by us – the human agents – through our interactions. It is a *created* reality in the sense that human mental contribution is vitally involved in the emergence of human society. We create social institutions, develop customs and languages, and legal systems, design cultural patterns in the mosaic of life, and so on. It is in this sense that human existence or social reality is the self-creation of humanity. Hence, the nature of this reality is essentially contrasted with that of physical reality. That is to say, human reality is not mind-independent in the way physical reality is. No mental contribution goes into the making of the natural occurrences of earthquakes, rainfall, or there being mountains, the sun and stars, light and darkness.

It is because of the mind-independent existence of physical reality that it is apt to expect or aim at detached *objective* knowledge or conception of this reality in and through natural-scientific enquiry. For here the search is for an account of reality as it objectively *is*, and not as it subjectively *appears* to be to any sentient being. Typically, a natural scientific account of some physical phenomenon contains a causal explanation of the phenomenon provided by reference to a specific law of nature. The natural law in question explains why a particular physical event occurs as the effect of some other event. All particular cause-effect relations are explained to be particular instances of a general type of physical regularity, which is what the law accounts for. And the regularities of nature are *brute facts*, just as particular physical events themselves are.

By contrast, human social reality cannot be regarded as consisting of brute facts. That there are social phenomena consisting of actions and interactions of human agents, who experience various feelings and emotions, and form hopes and ambitions, is not a brute fact in the way the fact that there are days and nights, stars and oceans, earthquakes and floods, is.

The reason for this difference is that social phenomena, being human phenomena, are imbued with *meaning* or significance. Whether it is a social institution, a family, friendship, a cultural product, a social movement, or the deprived human condition, the phenomenon has some human significance, both to the people who are directly affected by it and to others who are distantly concerned about it. Any social phenomenon is what it essentially is because self-conscious human agents view these phenomena as expressions of human motives, intentions and actions. Indeed, these *are* expressions of motives and intentions, desires and aspirations, actions and reactions. In the words of Wilhelm Dilthey, they are the 'objectifications of the mind'. And there is purposiveness built into the expressions of the mind. Human agency cannot be understood in non-purposive terms. Human actions are typically goal directed, and the goal or end is what the agent intends to achieve in the social world. Hence, the inter-subjective social reality of human actions and other attitudes is suffused with meaning for human agents or social beings.

Since social reality, unlike physical reality, is purposive in nature, the explanation of social phenomena is appropriately provided by reference to *reasons*, i.e., beliefs and desires, motives and intentions, rather than to causes. It is rational explanation, and not causal explanation, which is the proper mode of explaining purposive human actions. For purposiveness, with its meaningful content, is accountable in rational terms alone. And since human actions are structures with meaning and purpose, a social scientific explanation of them has to focus on the dimension of meaning that is the *reason* for doing the acts and the *value* attached to the fulfillment of the intention. A mere causal explanation typically provided in a natural scientific enquiry is inappropriate in social science, since such a form of explanation cannot accommodate the dimension of meaning and value.

One important reason why human social reality cannot be fully answerable to causal explanation of the kind given in natural science is that human beings and their social circumstances are all essentially *historical.* To say that an event has a cause is to say that there are universal laws, and to refer to initial conditions prevailing at particular times, such that given the law and a prevailing set of initial conditions, we can predict an event that is the effect of the cause. For example, given the general law: "At constant temperature and at low pressure, the volume of a given quantity of *any* gas is inversely proportional to the pressure exerted upon it", and the initial conditions, namely (i) the described experimental situation and (ii) the pressure of the gas increased by a measured amount, it follows, by natural necessity, that, other things being equal, the volume of the gas will be reduced proportionally to the exerted pressure. Similarly, given the general law that iron expands when it is heated, and given that the initial conditions X, Y, Z prevail, and that this is a case of iron being heated, we can make the prediction that iron will expand. Whether it is gas or iron, or stones or falling bodies, their behavior is strictly law-governed irrespective of time. The law-governed causal explanation is *ahistorical.* The past history of behavior of physical phenomena is scarcely part of their present situation.

By contrast, when we are dealing with human beings and their actions and attitudes, their past history is very much a part of their present situation. What kind of person we presently are is largely determined by our past, which can influence us so as to become, at times, very different sort of persons than what we were. Consequently, it is very difficult to know whether a given human case is really of a particular type that can be subsumed under a particular law we may have in mind. The case may very well be an exception to the presumed law. This historical contingency thus poses a inescapable problem to the possibility of typifying human beings and their actions for subsumption under socio-psychological laws.

Furthermore, the historical character of human beings also poses an inevitable problem for prediction of human actions in terms of regularity of their actions in the past. For example, a man who had offered alms to beggars whenever he came across one, might one day rebuke a beggar rather than give alms, because he might reflect on his past acts with regard to beggars and this self-reflective consideration could result in a break in the regularity of his past behavior in this regard. This is quite in contrast to physical phenomena, where past regularity in the behavior of an event or object is not similarly broken precisely because there is no question of the object's changing its behavior by any reflective consideration. This is why a natural scientist can better control and manipulate the physical phenomena for technological and other purposes. A natural scientific theory is not therefore threatened by any radical uncertainty and unpredictability of nature. But a social theory may not be so secure in the face of social reality. Revolutionary social changes do occur, and may seriously assail some highly respected social theory. Think of the breakdown of the Soviet Union and the fall of the Berlin wall.

We must be aware of the widespread view that the natural sciences can provide us with paradigms for the methods and procedures of social science. The very success of research in natural sciences seems to indicate that we have here the model or norm for science in general. But, our modelling the social sciences on the natural sciences reveals, on a closer scrutiny, our failure to recognize the distinctive feature of social reality and the corresponding peculiarity of *social theory* as against that of physical reality and physical theory. A physical theory gives us, among other things, a picture of underlying mechanisms or processes which explain the causal properties or powers of physical phenomena. We know, for example, that the kettle will heat up in contact with the fire; the kinetic theory will tell us what underlies heat transmission, so that we understand it as consisting more fundamentally in a transfer of kinetic energy. This explanatory theory is then put into practice to manipulate more effectively the features of our environment, and also to make predictions.

A social theory, on the other hand, cannot be conceived just in terms of descriptive, explanatory and predictive thinking. It cannot be a sufficient objective of a social theory that it just predict, or allow us to derive, the actual pattern of social and historical events, and the regularities which occur in human actions or event. A satisfactory explanation must also be such that it illuminates the purposive nature of self-conscious agents. The explanation must make *sense* of the agents. In other words, a social theory about some social practice or institution serves, beyond its explanatory and predictive purposes, to *define* social agents by making them understandable in terms of beliefs, desires, intentions and values making up in their world-view. For example, in a study of crime and violence, it is not enough that sociologists explore the relationship between incidents of violence, population density and poverty, and identify certain positive correlation between each of these variables. It would be an inadequate theoretical reflection, on the part of the sociologist, to view violence as a phenomenon in the external world that can be counted, measured, quantified and related to other material processes in society. The adequacy of this sociological study will not have been met until and unless an understanding of the participant agents is provided in terms of their *life-world*, that is how notions of *self and other, we and they*, prevail in the individual and collective psyche of the community.

Of course, to a certain extent, social theory is analogous to physical theory. An explanatory physical theory relates to practice in the sense that the theoretical knowledge of the underlying mechanisms is applied to cope better with physical reality. Social theory is also concerned with finding a more satisfactory fundamental description of what is happening in society. This tempts us to see social theory as offering an account of underlying processes and mechanisms of society, and as providing the basis of a more effective planning of social life. Here, the theory adds to, or alters, or replaces our pre-theoretical commonsense understanding of what is going on among the members of a society.

But there is a big *disanalogy*. A natural scientific theory relates to practice in an obvious way. There the relation of knowledge (theory) to practice is such that one applies what one knows about causal powers to particular cases. Practice is transformed by the application of theory, but the practice it transforms is not what the theory is about. It is in this sense external to the theory; the theory is about an independent object. For instance, knowledge of transfer of kinetic energy may be applied in such a way as to make our living condition more comfortable than what we could have afforded to do earlier. The earlier inconvenient practice gets transformed later by that application of knowledge or theory. But the practice in the context is not internally related to the theory or knowledge, because the theory is not *about* this practice. Rather, the practice that the theory transforms is an independent reality. One can accept the theory and, yet the practice can remain unchanged. For acceptance of the theory does not by itself result in transformation in practice: one may not wish or even decide to put the theory into practice.

It is this context of the relation of theory to practice that exposes the big disanalogy between natural science theory and social theory. Social theories are about *practices* in the sense that a society is, among other things, a set of institutions and practices. A social theory formulates explicitly the activity that is central to a practice, and articulates the norms that are essential to it. This formulation and articulation of a social practice may challenge, replace or extend society's pre-theoretical, commonsense understanding of that practice. It is these commonsense self-understandings of the practising participants that partially constitute the practice. A social theory about the practice is therefore explanatory of the *constitutive self-understandings* of the practice. We might say that it is a theory of *understanding the self-understandings* that partly constitute a social practice.

As such, accepting the (social) theory can itself transform the practice to the extent that the theory transforms participant's self-understandings. For instance, my acceptance of the Marxist theory of religion may alter my own earlier understanding of the practice of praying in a temple, where the practice is constituted by that self-understanding. In this way, theories in social sciences can undercut, bolster or transform the constitutive features of practices. Here, in contrast with natural sciences, acceptance of a theory *cannot* fail to influence, or have an effect upon, what the theory is about, namely the relevant practice. It is in this sense that the *object* of a social theory is not independent of, or external to, the theory.

7

An Ethno-Social Science for India

Towards Objectivity in Understanding

GURPREET MAHAJAN

In the social sciences, the critics of positivism emphasize the distinctiveness of the object of inquiry. They argue that the social reality is constituted through collective social action; hence, it is value-laden. In other words, values do not enter through the social scientist's investigation; rather they are already there in the object of inquiry. The absence of a rigid distinction between fact and value has led several theorists to conclude that the social sciences are improperly suited for scientific analysis; at least one cannot have objective knowledge in these disciplines.

Ethno-social science addresses itself to this predicament. While acknowledging the presence of values in the social domain, it argues that the social sciences do provide an objective understanding. In tendering this argument ethno-social science reformulates the notion of subject-object dichotomy: that is, it distinguishes between the historical world of the subject and the object, and from the aim, from the ethno-social perspective, it analyzes the object in terms of the values through which it is constituted. To put it a little differently, advocates of ethno-social science maintain that objectivity is jeopardized only when we impose our values on the object, and judge it through contemporary, and often incommensurate, set of norms.

Redefining objectivity in this manner, the ethno-social scientists suggest that we study the object through its own conceptual structure. Quite obviously, this methodology has gained considerable currency among social anthropologists, since they, more than others, are engaged in studying societies and cultures quite distinct from the advanced industrial societies to which its practitioners often belong. In recent times, McKim Marriott has attempted to construct an ethno-sociology for India. This paper examines this enterprise and seeks to determine whether a better or more objective understanding of India can emerge through this approach.

McKim Marriott writes: "Western societies often do not recognize and therefore cannot deal with the questions to which Indian institutions are an answer." To grapple with Indian questions and answers, we need a "social science of ideas that can be developed from the *realities known to Indian people.*"[1] Making a plea for an Indian ethno-social science, he says: "All social sciences develop from thought about what is known to particular cultures....It is an anomalous fact that social sciences used in India have developed from thought about the Western rather than Indian cultural realities..."[2] Consequently, they are unable to understand this society. To rectify this, we need to attend to "what is perceived by Indians in Indian categories"; we need to build from *"culture's natural categories."*[3] Marriott begins by acknowledging the need to discard western categories and patterns of classification. In fact, he insists that we expose ourselves to the other and understand it in its own terms. He assumes that there is an *Indian cultural reality* and an *Indian* way of making sense of that reality. The specific forms of social and political institutions existing here address questions that are peculiarly Indian. Consequently, how these institutions function and why they operate the way they do are questions that can be answered only by locating the "Indian mindset." He further assumes that the categories used by western sociologists – e.g., kinship, status, classes, social structure etc., – find no easy equivalent in the Indian mind. When we look for equivalents of these terms in rural India, we "...risk imposing an alien ontology and an alien epistemology upon those who attempt to answer."[4] We, therefore, need to abandon concepts and perceptions of western social science; instead we need to build from "culture's own categories."[5] The social scientist should "...synthesize a theoretical general system accompanying the realities known to Hindus, using both India's multiple textual sources and the evidence of its highly varied life."[6]

Thus, for Marriott, a legitimate and authentic reading entails the use of "culture's own categories." It implies, to take a different example, that the existence of village panchayats should not be equated with the existence of democratic institutional structure, if the culture does not itself describe these structures in that vocabulary. Similarly, the location of political and religious functions in different castes should not be represented by the term 'secularism', because such a term is alien to the culture itself. The voice of the culture is given primacy to ensure that we do not mis-read the other, or dismiss it "... for failing to resolve the western dilemmas in the modern manner."[7] It has the additional merit of ensuring that we do not minimize the differences between us and them by reading into the past, meanings and values that might not be present there. It also ensures that we do not confuse the existence of a few statements or signs with the existence of a coherent theory or cognitive apparatus.

The problem, however, is that it takes self-representation as an authentic and complete reading. It does not consider that the subjects may be mistaken in their beliefs and perceptions or that, points of view, external to that culture, may illuminate a dimension of reality that had remained unnoticed within the culture's self-representation. Worse still, it equates difference with incommensurability and assumes that no equivalence can be established between names and concepts. The existence of different "cultural realities" necessarily implies the existence of different rationalities and "cognitive categories."[8] Hence, indigenous concepts and definitions are regarded to be more appropriate; they are privileged unconditionally. By conceptualizing differences in this way, Marriott places the goal of knowing the other beyond the pale of understanding.

Understanding, one might add, begins with the immediacy of one's experience; what is outside the realm of experience cannot be fully understood. In any case, how can a finite consciousness transcend its own cultural world and open itself to the experience of another world, life and culture? How can cultural categories be accessible to people standing outside that tradition and way of life? How do we ensure that we hear the voice of the other without filtering it through pre-given categories and systems of classification available to us?

Marriott offers an answer to these questions. He maintains that employing culture's own categories can be one way of distancing ourselves from our prejudices. To register the voice of the other, he wishes to take the cultural leap; he hopes to become the other, and then seeks to perform the task that has, in his view, been neglected in the culture, namely, the establishment of an Indian ethno-social science. In allocating this task to himself, Marriott privileges the cultural *categories* but not the cultural *subjects*. By providing an ethno-social science, he wishes to correct the errors in contemporary Indian ways of analyzing the Indian reality. In other words, he wishes to be the 'authentic' Indian cultural voice; he neither accepts the existing cacophony of voices, nor does he maintain that the Hindus alone can understand or have access to Hindu categories. He assumes that others, outside the tradition, can have access to Hindu categories. The assumption is based perhaps on the belief that codified texts are available to all those who can read that language; that the cultural way of life is available to everyone who lives in that culture. Historicality of the subject is, in the process, neglected; in fact it is assumed that the meaning of texts is transparent; that they address us in a single voice; that our own cultural prejudices are simply biases that can be easily and self-consciously discarded.

While discussing Marriott's project of understanding and constructing an ethno-social science, it is perhaps important to mention that in the case of the former, he emphasizes the need to recover the "civilization's own categories"; while developing the latter, he suggests that we need to build a "general model of the culture studied." "A 'cultural interpretation' or a 'cultural account goes further towards systematizing: it takes indigenous words and concepts around Dilthey's 'hermeneutic circle' of meaning, building evocatively from the smaller local details to more general concepts..."[9] Accordingly, he provides, in his cubic representation of the principle of mixing, matching and marking, a theoretical framework for the organization of abstract categories of Hindu thought. The cube is expected to define "...the general semantic property space in which Hindus conceptually and perceptually dwell."[10] Writing about the structure of Nair house in Kerala, Moore says, "The three dimensional cube of the Hindu constituents offers a larger *conceptual framework* in which I found that I could *assemble* most of the manual's spatial formulations and relate both to the pattern of household activity that I had observed and to larger patterns of Hindu cosmology."[11] The adequacy of the principle offered in the cube is here being judged in terms of their ability to assist the ordering and classification of the available data. Its constituents are not present in this form in the Hindu cosmology.

Marriott assumes that his representation is merely a "... new generalized name intended to indicate some shared meanings and uses of the Sanskrit-named categories that it summarizes."[12] What he underestimates is that the schema adds a new dimension and a new set of properties that communicates more than what is incorporated in the Hindu categories that it seeks to systematize. For instance, "... the metonymic set of variables summarized as 'mixing,' 'marking' and 'unmatching' point respectively to the fundamental relational properties of mathematics and symbolic logic – reflexivity, symmetry and transitivity."[13] Here, the categories employed in the framework suggest more than a simple homology between aspects of Hindu thought, such as, fire and bile, water and phlegm. Indeed, it becomes a way of representing the Hindu mindset; it also suggests that self-reflexivity, transitivity, symmetry, and relations of equivalence that characterize contemporary western thought, are absent among the Hindus. One might also add that the framework devised by Marriott does not adequately represent the abstract categories that it seeks to systematize. While it establishes an equivalence between attachment (*kāma*) and passion (*rajas*), darkness (*tamas*) and incoherence (*adharma*), the suggested association of advantage (*artha*) with goodness (*sattva*) remains deeply unsatisfactory for the Hindu mindset.[14]

The inadequacy and the alienness of the schema are further evident from the fact that it sits uneasily upon many other readings of the Indian society. Raheja's analysis of mutuality and reciprocity of different castes in giving and receiving of *dan* (Hindu ritual of exchanging gifts) is read by Marriott as evidence of the principle of 'mixing' (non-reflexivity).[15] The right of the dominant caste to give and the obligation of other castes to receive certainly questions Dumont's principle of hierarchy, but it does not suggest that an entity in the Hindu world is "non self-sufficient to itself" or "incompletely related to itself, not even equivalent to itself – being to a greater or lesser degree open and dependent for its qualities and processes upon exchanges with others."[16] None of the features that define the principle of 'mixing' are the object of discussion in Raheja's analysis of inter-caste relationships. Similarly, the supremacy of the Gujjar caste in Pahansu challenges Dumont's placement of the Brahmin's at the top of the hierarchy and the related devaluation of the political and economic dimension, but it does not symbolize 'matching,' a principle that is described by Marriott as the relationship of transitivity.[17] Moore's analysis too makes a forced parallel when it associates the east-west dimension of the Nair household literally with the physical dimension of the opening of the house and mixing with the outside visitors, and 'matching' with the "messy operations" of giving birth, dying, grinding, cutting, cooking, feeding and eating.[18] If going beyond oneself is the essence of 'mixing,' then we can only make a distinction between actions and spaces that entail mixing and unmixing; we cannot, like Marriott, regard it as a characteristic specific to the Indian culture and different from the principle of reflexivity that informs the western civilization.[19]

While identifying 'unmixing' as an attribute of recent western popular thought and social science, Marriott suggests that it refers to a point of view where individuals are treated as "...indivisible, integrated, self-defining units, not normally subject to disjunction or reconstitution."[20] As we argued earlier, the mutuality of the relationships involved in the giving and receiving of *dan* does not entail disjunction or reconstitution. Nor does the carving out of space for different activities and sets of people (insiders and visitors) minimize the self-defined indivisible attribute of the individual. To take either of these activities as instances of 'mixing,' therefore, is to misrepresent the meaning that Marriott initially gives to these concepts. Assuredly, concepts are open to a variety of readings and authors cannot restrict the autonomy of the readers; yet, accentuating the 'culture's own voice' grants primacy to the author than the reader. For this reason, subsequent autonomy of readings, while being interpretatively justifiable, does violence to the position that Marriott defends and the project of ethnoscience that he and his associates in the book supposedly support.

Ignoring the inadequacies of the theoretical schema, what is important for the argument here is that metonymic variables represented by Marriott are not representations in culture's own voice. The general concepts offered are not of the same logical order as the smaller ones that embody the cultural voice. As such, while constructing an Indian ethno-social science, Marriott goes beyond culture's own representation and draws upon the resources available to him as an anthropologist trained in the western modes of thought. He cannot, despite his self-conscious efforts, discard the ways of thinking that shaped his historical consciousness.

Marriott stresses the need to distance oneself from the inherited western prejudices about India and Indian social reality. To this end, he tries to listen passively to the voice of the other without problematizing the act of reading and listening. That is, he fails to realize that the adequacy of understanding depends upon the manner in which the other is constructed. Consequently, the principles that govern the construction of the other are continuously ignored in his writings. Sometimes the debates in the field have misrepresented the case. Scholars have stressed the need to empathize with the other, to capture its authentic voice, and to forge an identity with it. Few, if any, have pointed out that the project of understanding depends upon the recognition of the differences between cultures; however, as a method of the study of *Geisteswissenschaften*, it entails an awareness of the historicity of the subject and the object. While it aims to capture the differences that underlie the various cultures, its distinctive attribute is its attempt to conceive the other as an historical entity.

The differences between cultures were recognized even by the Enlightenment; but in its enunciations, the difference (the other) was frequently designated as primitive, barbaric, and irrational: more importantly, it was represented as lacking a sense of historical and scientific thinking. The advocates of the method of hermeneutic understanding tried to rectify this perception; they tried to alter the Enlightenment rationality, particularly its attempt to present an essential dissimilarity between the self and the other. In its place, they postulated a fundamental similarity between the self and the other by treating both of them as historical entities, sharing universal conditions and attributes of being. By endowing all others with rationality and historicality, the advocates of understanding gave authenticity, respect, autonomy, and subjectivity to the other.[21] Contemporary attempts to understand cultures and civilizations, different from the western ones, have to be judged by this criterion; that is, by their ability to treat the other as an historical subject. Recognition of the differences *per se* or the recovery of indigenous categories is, in and by itself, insufficient.

Marriott's representation of the Hindu categories has frequently been challenged. What needs to be added to the existing critique is the recognition that he is unable to understand India or its social structure through the proposed schema, because the latter does not recognize the historicity of the other. Consequently, what emerges is an ahistorical and essentialist picture that is neither representative of any given past nor, for that matter, the present. This tendency is evident even in the general search for an essential Indian cultural form and the corresponding emphasis on the continuity of structures in the Indian civilization. Marriott assumes that the thought structure that informs individual action, patterns of kinship, family structure and social organization in India are, and have remained, fundamentally the same.

Marriott acknowledges the difference between the Indian and the western civilization; in fact, this distinction provides a justification for the project of ethno-social science. Further, while the difference between India and the West is recognized, no space is provided for internal differences. What we have, at the end of the analysis, is the essential form of particular institutions, and more generally, of the Indian culture. That latter is, in the main, identified with Hindu culture and recovered from the ancient Hindu texts. It is assumed that the purest and the most complete articulation of these values are to be found in the ancient Hindu texts, or religion. Hence, the classical texts are used to provide a framework in which ideas and patterns of belief are understood.

This mode of cultural representation has two implications: first, indology becomes a substitute for social science; in fact, one is easily confused with the other. Second, such an analysis is essentially reductionist and it supports the nineteenth century prejudices about the Orient. In the first instance, the complex system of internal and external organization that characterize the Indian society are reduced to the study of Indian culture, and the Indian culture becomes synonymous with the Indian tradition. Indian tradition is further read through the grid of codified, written texts and the texts used in the study are essentially classical Hindu texts of ancient India. Even there, only a few texts are taken into account. In Marriott's study, for instance, greater weightage is given to *Sāmkhya*; hence, we have statements such as: "Hindu thought generally following the ancient ideas of *Sāmkhya* assumes..."[22] while Hindu thought is associated with *Sāmkhya*, the latter is reduced to a triadic mode of presentation and argument. "...[T]here appears to be the irreducible number of properties or components with which Hindus will comfortably think about the human affairs."[23]

The political implications of this kind of reductionism that invariably accompanies the project of ethno-social science are quite serious. In one stroke, it grants legitimacy to the idea that the authentic Indian culture is Hindu culture; all other values and systems of thought become alien, secondary or subsidiary to it. On their own, they have no place in that which is 'authentically' Indian.

The element of dehistoricization is present in the very act of looking for an essential form. But this is not the only sphere in which it is manifest. It is apparent, more clearly, in Marriott's representation of India. While speaking of the West, Marriott refers to 'recent western popular thought and social science,' thereby suggesting a distinction between the present mode of thinking and that which preceded it. Thus, he assumes that ways of thinking have changed over a period of time in the West but not in India. Indeed, in Marriott's study, the West is read from the grid of the present: consequently, he finds presence of equivalence thinking present in the West since the Greek times. However, when it comes to India, he reverses the strategy. The present Indian society is analyzed from the grid of the past. It is the categories embodied in ancient Hindu texts that are taken as the defining features of the Hindu/Indian universe. Thus, we are told that "...the constructs explored here may be as much for the present and future as for past Hindu and wider worlds."[24]

Besides the fact that such an analysis precludes the possibility of any serious engagement with the present, it also helps to rehearse and reinforce some of the dominant beliefs about the Orient. It associates change with western civilization and stasis with India. This representation of the self and the other reinforces the image of the West as an historical civilized space and condemns India and other non-western societies to the inescapable prison of an eternal and everlasting past. As a consequence, India becomes a society marked by stratification, hierarchy, non-reflexivity, non-transitivity and non-symmetrical relations; a society where "...persons are composite, divisible (what one might call 'dividuals')..."[25] As a matter of contrast, we are told that in the West "...persons and many other entities are postulated as being normally self-reflexive (individuals having an identity with and being sufficient in themselves), and as symmetrical (equal) and transitive (consistent) in their relationship with each other...Given such units, inter-personal influences, inequalities and changes have to be brought in as external factors or pathologies."[26] Since Hindus are seen to be people who are "not necessarily identical with or otherwise related only to themselves," "not necessarily equal" and "not necessarily consistent," it follows logically that they must, or should accept a mode of organization quite different from that of the modern West. To put it more sharply, liberal democracy and the institutional structures, supported by individualism and egalitarian attitudes, become alien and unnatural for it. The struggle of the Indian people for self-governance, democracy and individual rights is thus effaced, or at least relegated to the margins of Indian history.

Understanding, as it was argued earlier, is essentially an attempt at reading a text – a culture, civilization, practice or a written document – historically. Being aware of the historicity of the author, the original context and addressee, it is aware of the possibility of different readings located in different historical time and space. Even when it tries to reconstruct the author's intended meaning, it refers to the meaning assimilated by the contemporaries of the author. Thus it remains aware of the possible contexts of meaning. And in the study of codified texts, it recognizes the relative autonomy of the reader as well as the relative autonomy of the subjects who incorporate these ideas and values in their life system. It works, in other words, with a different conception of culture. It assumes that the text of a culture is creatively read by its people; hence, unlike Marriott, it does not suggest a simple correspondence between a given text and the practices it informs.

To conclude, the inadequacies of Marriott's enterprise arise from a misconception of the act of understanding. What we need to remember is that an adequate and objective understanding can emerge only when the principle of historicity is applied to the self and the other. If this dimension is absent in the construction of the other, then our understanding of it will be neither adequate nor objective.

Notes

1. McKim Marriott, "Constructing an Indian Ethnosociology," in M. Marriott (ed.), *India Though Hindu Categories*, Delhi: Sage, 1990, p. 1.
2. ibid.
3. ibid. (emphasis added).
4. ibid., p. 2.
5. ibid., pp. 4-5.
6. ibid., p. 6.
7. ibid.
8. ibid., p. 4.
9. ibid.
10. ibid., p. 23.
11. M. A. Moore, "The Kerala House as a Hindu Cosmos" in M. Marriott (ed.), *India Through Hindu Categories*, Delhi: Sage, 1990, p. 191.
12. Marriott, op cit., p. 16.
13. ibid., p. 17.
14. ibid., p. 13.
15. ibid., p. 26. See also, G.G. Raheja, "Centrality, Mutuality and Hierarchy: Shifting Aspects of Inter-caste Relationships in North India," in M. Marriott (ed.), *Indian Through Hindu Categories*, Delhi: Sage, 1990.
16. ibid., p. 19.

17. ibid., p. 17 and also p. 20.
18. Moore, op cit., pp. 192-95.
19. Marriott, op cit., p. 17.
20. ibid., p.17.
21. Gurpreet Mahajan, *Explanation and Understanding in the Human Sciences*, Delhi: Oxford University Press, 1992, pp. 50-73.
22. Marriott, op cit., p. 21.
23. ibid., p. 28.
24. ibid., p. 33.
25. ibid., p. 21.
26. ibid., p. 28.

II

Culture and Tradition

8

Tradition as Narrative

RAJAN GURUKKAL

It is not easy to define what tradition means though there are a number of definitions available in the sociological and anthropological textbooks.[1] All of us know that the term refers to the aggregate of what is underlying and significant as historically contingent in the ways of life of a culturally bound land and people. Taken in a larger ethnographic sense, tradition refers to the complex aggregate of morals, normative values, conventions, customs, rituals, laws, beliefs, arts, and knowledge. An overt expression of these will not help us define the term. On the contrary, it is the covert dimension of the complex whole that signifies tradition. One is born in one's tradition and inherits it. Despite the fact that a child starts imbibing the tradition through socialization, it is essential that one is born into it and no one can ever be a convert into a tradition. Conversion through proselytizing religions does hardly ever supplant the original tradition. No one can concretize its meaning that is metaphorical. It denotes a transcendental syntactic structure that is elusive, if approached ontologically. It is hard to objectively characterize a people's tradition either by themselves who are inside it, or by others who are outsiders.

As a consciously articulated entity, tradition is a narrative – an imagined text of the absolute and the transcendent that is uncritically accepted by a people as their inheritance from the past. A tradition, approximated as common to several societies or the people of a sub-continent, is imaginary and can very well be called an invention.[2] It is the making of a consolidated vision about one's heritage, an emotive attempt of fabrication around the images of the past. The people at a crucial juncture construct their tradition from the fragments of history and believe it as a grand discovery of truth about them. This is done at the insistence of tradition, pure, absolute and transcendent that denies comprehension beyond textuality. Hence, it acts as the absent cause of the narrated. The incomprehensible and absoluteness about tradition is inevitably absent in every text, though it facilitates textualization.[3] Hence the texts are proofs of failed attempts at capturing what tradition is. Textualized or imagined tradition transcends internal contradictions that are historically contingent. The people seldom feel the inner conflicts of a tradition.[4]

A narrative restoration of the lived tradition becomes inevitable for a people implicated in a relationship of confrontation between themselves and the colonizing other.[5] Textualization of tradition becomes necessary in a society where an identity crisis sets in at the instance of an imposing alien culture as the other. It is the transformingly influencing presence of the other, poised in a relationship of confrontation with the self, that necessitates the construction of one's identity. It is an act of resistance expressed through the construction of cultural self-differentiation by a people. It is impossible for a people to be conscious of the tradition as long as they are subsumed by it, and there is no need to be conscious of it either. Tradition becomes an object of knowledge only in a situation of external challenge, wherein the self is confronted by an indomitable other. Often the representation by the other triggers traditional self-consciousness and the inevitable self-alienation, making one turn the face to oneself and recognize tradition.

Tradition as a sociological category is analytically accessible and hypothesizable today as only against the meanings and measures of modernity. We recognize tradition in the opposition to modernity.[6] So, the history of people's consciousness about tradition cannot be older than the beginnings of modernity. The rise of modernity co-temporal with the rise of tradition. The birth of traditionality manifest in the act of conscious articulation of tradition has always been a direct outcome of the confrontation with modernity. In this sense, the Indian tradition became understandable only when it was represented in the western diction as an object different from and in relation to the colonial modernity, an expression invoked here as a summative metaphor to denote the nineteenth century western worldview. The people of India became conscious of their tradition in the process of colonial de-traditionalization or modernization.[7] The colonial modernity acted as the provocation for the people to think about themselves as Indians with a sense of tradition.

The colonial representation of Indian tradition helped the colonized to search for their tradition. This mode of perceiving tradition, though appeared to be a reaction to the western worldview, was entirely non-traditional and modelled on the Orientalist imagination.[8] What was interesting about the process was the transformation of the relationship of confrontation or resistance into a *game* with the other. The other that set the rules of the game naturally became the model for the self to reconstruct itself, and consequently the self got modernized unknowingly.[9] Though ostensibly a conscious move towards traditional restoration, in effect it turned out to be modernization. What was perceived as tradition was actually modernity, and what the act replicated as tradition was the western perception of the Indian past.

This is not to argue that none of the pre-modern societies had ever been conscious of their traditions in any form. Some kind of consciousness of tradition was present in all societies since each of them did distinguish itself from the rest with a sense of self and the other. Traditions and traditional consciousness were definitely pre-modern, but what is coeval with modernity is traditionality manifest in its textual objectification. It is not the type of primordial consciousness discernible in pre-modern societies, but a full-fledged one capable of treating tradition as an object. Textual description, characterization, classification, definition, and interpretation of tradition cannot arise from the simple level of consciousness. It would require a certain level of alienation from the tradition to objectify it through texts. Therefore, it is anachronistic to ascribe traditionality to pre-modern societies wherein people were totally subsumed by the tradition. Before we go further, it is important to draw the distinction between the ancient and modern levels of consciousness of tradition a little more clearly.

Tradition as the lived life of a given people and tradition as their self-image will have to be differentiated as two separate entities. The former is natural, transcendental, and hardly amenable to textualization. The latter is a self-articulated version of the former, and an endogenous aspect of any descent group in a relationship of confrontation with similar other groups. Every group acquires a self-image in the process of its relating to and distinguishing of itself from the rest. In the same process, every group draws an image of the other through observation. In both the cases, the former is the absent cause. The self-image, though gets sharpened against its counterpart, is sometimes overshadowed by the other in a state of continued subjection. The subjected people unconsciously reconstruct their self-image exactly as constructed by the subjugator.

There is no terminological differentiation to indicate the separation between tradition as self-image and lived reality. In the Indian subcontinent, the terminological counterpart of tradition could be many, but summatively, *paramparā* in the Indo-Aryan and *valimura* in the Dravidian stand out referring to tradition centered around the *gotra, gaṇa, kula, jana* and *jāti*. The tradition of a descent group is called a *kathā*, narration in the diction of orality. Complex societies integrating diverse descent groups into larger wholes required macro-traditions subsuming the micro-ones and linking peoples and places in a wider terrain. The *itihāsa* genre of tradition centering around *janapadas* exemplifies a macro model integrating numerous micro *kathās* or micro-traditions. There are other subsequent genres like *Puraṇas* and *Caritas* of disparate periods encapsulating traditional consciousness in societies of political polarities, economic differentiation, and hierarchical stratification necessitating construction of imagined macro-traditions. They draw upon the traditional consciousness in myths, epics, genealogies and chronicles, emphasizing in the first place the *Vamsa caritas,* which is inevitable in a society weighing the factors of *varṇa* and *jāti* for status, ranking, and authority.[10]

Micro-traditions are syncretically united and synthesized into a macro-tradition over the years under the influence of historical forces. It is a gradual process resulting from the co-existence and interaction of micro-traditional people who, in due course, come under structures of dominance. One macro-tradition eventually becomes central and decisive in the act of synthesizing of the rest for the making of a macro-tradition, the mechanisms of which are certainly complex and hardly schematic. In the case of India, micro-traditions were synthesized by the brāhmanical and heterodox religious worldviews with varying ranges of social control under different periods.[11] The former received a relatively more extensive influence as the hegemonic macro-tradition in later years. But these worldviews themselves had never been coherent, since continuous assimilation of local traditions and the corresponding reconstruction from within kept the macro-traditions as new wine in old bottle.

The case that the Indian tradition is a historiographic construct and not historical one is yet to be made out. It is essential here to briefly survey the historical processes and juxtapose the construct of Indian tradition against them. The Indian subcontinent has always been inhabited by unevenly evolved people with different cultures and traditions. From the antiquities of simple self-sustaining descent groups to the years of complex societies and their co-existence and interaction, acculturation and assimilation, a broad matrix of common tradition did take shape out of the long processes of shared cultural practices of continuity and change. The sociologists have called it 'the great tradition' or *mārgī* as distinguished from the 'little traditions' or *desi.*[12] The major strands of the *mārgī* can be traced back to the Vedic, *ithihāsic, sāstraic* and *purāṇic* ways of life. But both the *mārgī* and *desi* were constantly being reconstructed under the transforming influence of one upon the other and *vice versa.*

The relatively simple tradition of Vedic pastoral tribes nuanced over the centuries became extremely complex as the people migrated to the Gangetic region and turned into settled agriculturists. A spate of new ideologies shook their traditions around the sixth century B.C., of which the effect of Jainism and Buddhism were the most traumatic and fundamental. The protests of Jain and the Buddhist orders against the brahmanical beliefs, rituals, and the *varṇa* system of social stratification are well attested by the canonical texts. The predatory marches and further migrations from within and without added to the reconstructive influence on traditions. Ideologies of dissent and protest against the brahmanical tradition got ramified along the atheistic orders of *Cārvākas, Bārhaspatyas* and *Kaulas.*

In the wake of the socio-economic transformations, the heterodox ideologies themselves underwent major changes and got reconstructed more or less in the idioms of pre-existing traditions. A new social formation characterized by the drying up of long distance trade and urban centers, heralded. expansion of localized agrarian village economy, hierarchically structured land relations, proliferation of rigid caste groups of hereditary occupations, and crystallization of a subject peasantry. New ideologies and sensibilities followed, of which *Bhakti*, the cult of self-surrender, was the most significant reconstructive force as far as tradition was concerned. The ideology of *bhakti* as enunciated in the epic and *purāṇic* compositions like *Gitā*, *Harivanśa*, *Bhāgavata* and *Viṣṇu Dharmottara*, mirroring not only the conditions of human existence, but also the way people were made to live the contradictory social relations, radically reconstituted the pre-existing tradition. In the Gangetic heartland and central India, *bhakti* spread through *Bhāgavata-Nārāyaṇa* cult to begin with and *Nārāyaṇa-Viṣṇu cult subsequently*.[13] It spread towards the lower Ganges through the cult of *Nārāyaṇa-Vāsudeva* and *Sankarṣaṇa* and all over the continent as the cult of *Viṣṇu*. The new religious sensibility of *bhakti*, particularly the syncretic pervasiveness of *Viṣṇu-bhakti*, cultivated extensively in the land through temples and texts, laid the foundations of a macro-tradition along the agrarian villages of comparable social structures.

The cult of *bhakti* took a different institutional form and swept through the deeper South towards the sixteenth century. It emerged as a movement of temples with *Śiva* or *Viṣṇu* as deities, led by hymnists of the *Nayanar* and *Alvar* traditions.[14] The ideology and social context were the same as in the North. It was the period of localized agrarian expansion, hierarchical structuring of social relations, and crystallization of the caste system in the region. Compared to the master code of *bhakti* formulated in the *Purāṇas* and the *Gītā*, the South Indian *bhakti*, expressed in the devotional songs of *Nalayira devyaprabhandam, Tevarm, Tiruvācakam* and *Tirukkovaiyār*, is more simple, emotional and personal. Naturally, it was much more appealing. The most striking difference was its shift from the abstraction of *Purāṇas* and the *Gītā* to personalization. Certain *Śaiva* monastic orders, like the *Kāpālikas, Pāśupatas*, and *Kālāmukhas*, emerged in the seventeenth century as deviants from the temple traditions and directed against the brahmanical tradition. They advocated a free society of sexual license and alcoholism in contradistinction to the brāhmanical morals and preached tantricism. There emerged several other saivite sects, like the *Dasanāmi sanyāsis* modelled on the heterodox *sanghas*. Remarkably different from all the previous *śaiva* monastic orders, a new *śaiva* sect, namely the *Viraśaivas*, emerged around the twelfth century, vigorously questioning the priestly supremacy of the Brahmins. Corresponding to the developments on the *śaiva* monastic orders, several Vaiṣṇava sub-sects belonging largely to the *Pancarātra* cult also emerged. This is not something peculiar to the South. All over the subcontinent, the sects and sub-sects proliferated as traditions, counter traditions and reconciliations.

Asceticism, often pointed out as a salient feature of the Indian tradition, did persist over the centuries, at times as individual practices and at other times as a group cult, among those who congregated around certain individual ascetics. The cult of self-renunciation and the leading life of ideological closure and austerity were always present, but on an extremely small scale compared to the number of saints in Europe. Most of them transmitted the message of conciliatory ethic and discharged an ameliorative function in times of tension either through a worldview of pacifism or dedication of themselves to the cause of suffering. There is no uniformity about the ascetic traditions in India. Austerity, celibacy, and total seclusion are the universals in the ascetic way of life everywhere in the world. One cannot identify an Indian model of asceticism which varied from the *parivrājaka, snātaka, bikṣu* types to the *avadhūta, jñāni* types and so on, constituting a wide range of traditions with different levels of renunciation and partial or full or no social contact.

Totally distinct from the earlier ascetic traditions and the *bhakti* cult, a devotional movement of the common people with elements of dissent and protest spread throughout the core region during the immediate modern period. It threw up a number of saints of the *Santa* tradition, committed to work against social ills, religious obscurantism, and complex ritualism. A complex structure of agrarian relations based on a variety of tenurial categories, militaristic obligations, administrative responsibilities, and sacerdotal privileges resting on subjected artisans, crafts folk, peasantry, and other servile people, organized into a rigid caste system characterized contemporary society. Trade, urban development, increased monetarization and a strong state system made the life of the poor full of oppression and exploitation. The *Santa* waves of protest and reform swept through the lower order of the society, thus opening up a space for a popular religion. It was a counter-traditional movement directed against the priestly domination in contemporary brāhmānical Hinduism.

Islam as an independent macro tradition has a long history in the sub-continent, embracing numerous micro traditions of age-old beliefs and customs. Many an aspect of local micro traditions has become ingrained in it. Islamic tradition in India hardly escaped certain aspects of other micro traditions that were transformed into components of the brāhmānical macro tradition; for instance, the institution of lineage, caste and hierarchical ranking. These two macro traditions have always been influencing each other despite the historiographic divide that colonial rule intentionally perpetrated and nurtured to the extent of turning them into combating polarities. Now the historiographic divide is being carried forward as a strategy of exclusion for the construction of *Hindutva*, on the one side, and the corresponding identity construction through Islamisation on the other.[15] When the nation of a partly uprooted and culturally misrepresented people, who are victims of colonial rule, comes to claim political power, the processes at both ends turn out be naturally fundamentalist and rigorous in terms of traditional self-reconstruction

What emerges from the survey of historical antecedents is a scenario of traditional plurality, where multiple traditions coexisted, interacted and influenced one another. There is more discontinuity than continuity, and reconstitution than persistence, of traditions. It is impossible to discover a historically contingent single macro-tradition of continuity and change out of the multitude, however meticulous we are in our search for a common core. Formation of macro-traditions took place at different points of time as and when facilitated by structures of domination in wider social formations. But all of them underwent radical transformations too. However, one might succeed in imagining the Indian tradition as a source of unity within the diversity of traditions in a mode of philosophical perception and appreciation. But it is a construct – a construct contingent upon the nation state.

The making of Indian tradition had been an exogenous articulation enabled under colonialism. It was at first the effect of the representation of the colonized by the colonizer, and subsequently, as a sequel to it, in the form of the image the people sought about themselves exactly as construed by their colonial masters. Initially, we see the tradition constructed through the writings of Orientalists, Indologists, and imperialists, who contemplated it dichotomously as a cultural bifurcation into Aryan and Dravidian. Orientalism provided the knowledge base for the construct that acquired the elements of its structure from the concept of stagnant village communities, despotism, non-revolting, non-reforming social type, the Aryan theory and the notion of a religiosity based on renunciation.

The Indian tradition erroneously epitomized as Hinduism is a structured outcome of colonial imagination. It is a grand narrative that grew up incorporating representations in the translations and commentaries of Vedic and Purāṇic and Śāstraic texts, imperial gazetteers, census reports and other Indological writings of the colonial period. The later Indologists, sociologists, historians and anthropologists, through their studies on language, race, caste and religion, made the narrative more specific within the same old knowledge system of orientalism. What was lost sight of were the plurality and diversity of traditions, ranging from theism and theistic atheism to atheistic theism and materialism. There may be no nation like India that had to suffer so much from misrepresentation. The German and French had a leading role, though inadvertently, in perpetuating a false image of Indian culture – the spiritual image. All the European indologists replicated the same caricature. The false image easily went deep into the colonial Indian mind that internalized its history only as told by the westerners. Accepting their colonizability as natural and seeking to modify themselves according to the mirror image of the colonizer, the Indians took many of the western sarcastic attributions, like the characteristic inwardliness, religiosity and spirituality as matters of pride. They not only sought truth about their heritage in the western misrepresentations, but also began to live by them, enabling quite a few outstanding sages to appear in modern India.

The indigenous textualization of tradition commensurate with the reification of the master narrative has given rise to two ideologically distinct versions: one providing cultural basis for *nationalism*, and the other justifying *revivalism*. The ideological differences apart, the overall characterization of tradition remains the same in both the versions as affective responses of the colonized to the self-images they borrowed from the colonizer. They were characterized, more or less, by the perspectives of Orientalism with the nineteenth century value supplements such as the western utopia of progress, welfare and egalitarianism and a rational outlook.

The reduction of the Indian tradition by modern sociology into certain cognitive-structural attributes such as hierarchy, holism, continuity and transcendence is not entirely free from the prison house of the colonial mode of comprehension. The evolutionist treatment stressing the systematic increase of differentiation and structuration has not helped. So much so that even the functionalist approach did not quite serve the purpose. The structuralist studies and materialistic interpretations or its substantivist diversifications seldom succeed in bringing about any fundamental change in the perception of tradition. The sociological perspectives and their analytical strategies were, by and large, guided by the western ideas of religion, community and social stratification. The post-modern approaches are equally entrenched in the inescapable westernism, and certainly do not provide for a non-European paradigm. But they do generate useful insights and intellectual strategies of decolonization, though the lurking danger of they themselves turning into traps of neo-colonization remains. Their linguistic invasion and conceptual colonization are indeed outrageous, but the built-in methodological potential of critical self-reflexivity does hopefully counter-balance the danger.

Notes

1. Tradition denotes a set of inner-related cultural traits lasting for a longer time span. It encompasses values, norms, beliefs, customs, rituals, cosmology, eschatology, and knowledge transmitted from generation to generations by a people. There are various definitions, but all of them remain more or less clinging on to the kernel: the

uncritically accepted collective belief. For a nuanced version of tradition, see Lloyd I. Rudolph and S.H. Rudolf, *The Modernity of Tradition*, Delhi, 1967.

2. The basic concepts are drawn from Benedict Anderson, *Imagined Communities*, London, 1983. Also, the 'Introduction' by Hobsbawm and T. Ranger, eds., *The Invention of Tradition*, Cambridge, 1983, pp. 1-2. For a detailed consideration of these concepts in the case of a related issue and directly relevant context, see Romila Thapar, "Imagined Religious Communities: Ancient History and Modern Search for a Hindu Identity," in her *Interpreting Early India*, New Delhi, 1993, pp. 60-88.
3. This is a situation similar to the case of relationship between history and historical texts. History as absolute past is the cause of all historical texts, but keeps itself off from every one of them. For a discussion of history as an absent cause of written history, see Althusser, *Reading Capital*, London, 1970, pp. 199-308.
4. For the concept of inner conflict of tradition, see J.C. Heesterman, *The Inner Conflict of Tradition*, Delhi, 1985, pp. 43ff.
5. See the discussions in Albert Memmi, *The Coloniser and the Colonised*, Boston, 1967. Relevant concepts are formulated in Edward Said, *Orientalism*, New York, 1985. See also his *Culture and Imperialism*, London, 1993, pp. 230-260.
6. For a different treatment transcending the usual dichotomy between modernity and tradition, see Lloyd I. Rudolph and S.H. Rudolph, *The Modernity of Tradition, op. cit.*, Introduction, pp. 3-14. The argument that there exists no binary opposition between the two is certainly acceptable, though not exactly as it is made out to be in Rudolphs. In fact, it is not the opposition that is unreal, but, on the contrary, what is assumed to be the tradition. Modernity and tradition are indeed two different things. At the same time, a tradition is no longer a visible unless juxtaposed against modernity that is its expressive causality.
7. For an extended discussion on related issues, see Ashis Nandy, *Intimate Enemy: Loss and Recovery of Self Under Colonialism*, New Delhi, 1983. Also Partha Chatterjee, *The Nation and its Fragments*, Delhi, 1994, pp. 95ff.

8. It is the representational knowledge on India generated by European Indologists that we invoke here. For a study of the Indological characterization of India's past, see Romila Thapar, "Indology and Interpretation of Early Indian History," in her *Interpreting Early India, op. cit.*, pp. 1-22. An elaborate analysis of 'orientalism' as a historically accumulated corpus of western knowledge about the east is given in Edward Said, *Orientalism, op.cit.*

9. The insights are drawn from the analytical categories like 'discourse' and 'subject' developed in the works of Michel Foucault. See Colin Gorden (ed.), *Power/Knowledge*, New York, 1980. Also see Michel Foucault, *Archeology of Knowledge*, New York, 1982

10. See the analysis of the relevance and significance of genealogy in a society attaching great importance to jati and varna attempted in Romila Thapar, "Society and Historical Consciousness: The Ithihasa-Purana Tradition," in her *Interpreting Early India, op. cit.*, pp. 137-173.

11. M.N. Srinivas, *Social Change in Modern India*, California, 1966, pp. 1-52. Also see the historical overview of the orthogenetic processes of Indian tradition in Yogendra Singh, *Modernization of Indian Tradition*, New Delhi, rept, 1977, pp. 28-59. Also the discussion on the macro-structural changes, ibid., 122-129.

12. The concept is promulgated in Robert Redfield, "The Social Organization of Tradition," *Far Eastern Quarterly*, Vol. 15, 1955-56, pp. 13-21. Also see the Introduction in Milton Singer, *Traditional India: Structure and Change*, Philadelphia, 1959, pp. 10-12.

13. For a detailed historical analysis of the spread of the Vaiṣṇava bhakti, see Suvira Jaiswal, *The Origin and Development of Vaiṣṇavism*, rept. New Delhi, 1981, pp. 116-122.

14. For a comprehensive analysis of the Tamil bhakti movement, see M.G.S. Narayanan and Veluthat Kesavan, "Bhakti Movement in South India," in S.C. Malik (ed.), *Dissent, Protest and Reform in Indian Civilization*, Shimla, rev. edn., 1980.

15. Recently there has appeared a number of studies on this subject. Perhaps the most rigorous analysis of the issue is done in Muralidharan, "Community Formation, Colonial Habitus and the Brahmanical Lifeworld," in *Haritam, Journal of School of Letters*, Mahatma Gandhi University, No. 7, 1996.

9

Understanding Indian Culture

The Question of its Unity and Identity

G.C. PANDE

Culture cannot be said to inhere in any particular community as its inseparable form or property. As a mode of the human awareness of values, it is acquired through the educational and symbolic tradition of the society in which it finds expression. Now, while society acquires reality through human individuals and culture acquires reality through society, it is nevertheless true that individuals find their identity from society from its culture. Thus, although as a mode of consciousness the identity of a culture is revealed by its own innate features and structures, its existence and continuity in space and time depend upon the vitality of the tradition of symbols and education in a historically existing society.

To which Indian community or communities does Indian culture belong? This question, though often asked, is an ill-phrased one. This is so because it is assumed that a culture can be identified simply by pointing to a community as existing at any given moment of time. Such a procedure fails to take into its account that no historical society is homogenous and that the ideal symbolic world of a culture has a relative autonomy. The Pythagorean theorem, for instance, is not something that can be said to belong to an individual personality; it cannot be regarded as the property or as under the power of a particular individual named Pythagoras. On the other hand, it is a truth seen and expressed by Pythagoras in a particular manner. But the content of this discovery may be acquired and formulated by any qualified person and it may be known in different forms in different ages. Only as a particular expression of a universal truth is it historically linked with Pythagoras. Similarly, geometry as a theoretical system based on axiomatic reasoning and illustrated diagrams is remembered as an achievement of the ancient Greeks. At the same time, it is pointless to ask how many or which Greeks actually share in it today. What is true of science is more or less true of religion, art and other branches of higher culture. Even symbols, games, customs and fashions may spread far and wide and lose contact with their places of origin.

Culture as the apprehension of values has a basic cognitive dimension. As an ideal it has an universal relevance. Nevertheless, this universally shareable and estimable aspect of culture assumes different forms in the course of its symbolic expression in historical traditions. On different levels of understanding and in different domains of action it appears in diverse forms. The identity of a culture is thus to be recognized through its symbols as expressive of a tradition of self-consciousness and in terms of the purely behavioral, ethnic or material characteristics of those who illustrate it.

The unity of a culture is not the unity of any social unit in terms of ethnic substance or structure. It is of the same kind as the unity of self-consciousness that is able to define any object in relation to itself and locate it within the circumference of its world. How wide the circumference and how deep the unity of a culture are, depend on the catholicity of the mind informed by it.

They do not depend on external circumstances. For a person with a catholic outlook, culture is basically *world* culture.

Those savants of the last century who perceived the unity of Indian culture accepted its catholic outlook that regarded all religions as streams leading towards one and the same ocean. This perspective of the *unity of all faiths* constitutes the identity of Indian culture, not the historical stages of its embodiment in civilization. Cultures, however, are not separate, homogenous entities that may be counted in the same manner in which population is counted. Just as many and manifold social units combine to form a macro-society, a number regional, ethnic, and factional sub-cultures combine to form the great tradition as a macro-culture. For example, the peoples of diverse regions like Kashmir, Kerala or Ladakh, of diverse tribes like the Santhals and Nagas, of diverse faiths like the Sikhs and Muslims, and of diverse classes or groups like the priests and craftsmen, the educated and the illiterate, the rich and the poor, all enter into the fold of *Indianness* without abandoning any of their distinguishing features.

The basic formula of Indianness is to 'live and let live.' It has never sought to force the tribal ways of life into any pre-determined standard model, nor has it sought to push different religious communities into one single and straight path. In all of them, it has seen the same pervasive truth that cannot be described, but to accept which one must abandon one's limited ego and egoistic interests. It requires that all the accepted content of one's life should be regarded merely as an accident or symbol, and that through this understanding their hold on the ego gets loosened which, in turn, reduces one's separation from others. Beyond the common life of the world, but situated near the heart, is the profound truth that constitutes the ultimate goal of man. Man has to seek it with the help of the wise, though the path is not fixed. This belief is common to all traditions in different measures. The consciousness of this truth is the consciousness of Indian culture.

Some scholars have, after much research, presented certain examples of intolerance, fanaticism or violence in the name of religion in Indian history. They have also tried to prove that the realty of Indian life is very far from its spiritual ideals. From this they have concluded that the so-called tolerant and spiritual character of Indian culture is mythical and false. Doubtless, if such is the case, then the unity and the perennial character of Indian culture must also be regarded as imaginary, and in the place of Indian culture one should speak of accidental and miscellaneous collections of facts – different languages and religions, modes of living, geographical and other ethnic facts.

In reply to this, it may be stated that in the area of religious conflict the proved instances of intolerance and violence in Indian history appear as exceptional, and exceptions tend to prove the rule. Again, it is not being argued that the Indian ideal of religious tolerance implies that the ordinary Indian has a nobler character than men have in other cultures, just as the rationality of the Greek culture did not mean that the average Greek was more rational than the average Persian. It only means that Indian savants have often explained religious truth from a catholic perspective and that the Indian rulers have often followed the policy of religious tolerance.

As far as the factual diversity is concerned, it does not contradict the unity apprehended in *ethical consciousness* at the highest level. Culture is not simply dependent on material and hedonistic pursuits. Such pursuits are necessarily involved in the conflict of self-interests. To a mind that is centered on the ego and turned towards the maximization of satisfactions, it would be hard for a sense of equality between one self and another to arise and endure. In reality, social justice requires an elevated moral sense and that ultimately requires the knowledge of spiritual equality. One must identify Indian culture in terms of its spiritual practice. But this does not imply that religion and morality as currently practiced in the Indian society have always been consistent with this spiritual ideal. In cultural history, the quest for realization of ideals can never be claimed as a completed process. In this sense, the ideal of Indian culture may be said to be essentially the ideal knowledge for which the sages aspired. Nevertheless, it is the essence of all cultures to seek the best. Its essence is not constituted by the actuality of average life, but by the ideal aspired for.

Some modern scholars have described the Indian mind as irrational or non-rational, because they find that the Indian thought is cluttered with inconsistent and unanalyzed concepts. It has also been suggested that this is the result of the fact that the Indian mind represents that stage of evolution when reason was not yet fully developed. Doubtless, there has been an evolution of rational knowledge, but there is no evidence for the evolution of the rational faculty. On the contrary, the very fact that there was a development of rational knowledge destroys the hypothesis of the evolution of the rational faculty. In the absence of the rational faculty, how can rational knowledge evolve? Most of the social and cultural institutions of man go back to prehistoric times for their origin. But the prehistoric man was never at a loss in dealing with his natural environment for satisfying his needs through manipulation. In this context, it is interesting to recall a charge that Ludwig Wittgenstein leveled against J.G. Frazer, the author of *The Golden Bough*. He remarked: "Fraser is far more savage than the savage races because those savages were not so far from understanding spiritual matters as an English man of the 20th century."

As examples of such irrational thought, ritual incantations, spiritual beliefs and omens, rebirth, caste, etc. have been cited. It has been said that the eradication of this irrationality is a part of the process of modernization. In reality, rituals are part of the system of worship. The objects or actions employed in it do not function in their natural capacity, but only in their symbolic capacity. They are employed as prescribed by the *Śāstras* and serve a transcendental purpose. The basis of rituals is not the laws of empirical causality. As far as the use of *mantras* or *tāntric* practices or astrology is concerned, belief in them is supported by practical experience. Belief in omens is common, and universal too. The proof for the principles of *Karma* and rebirth lies in the scriptures and the words of the savants. Restrictions on social contact are ritualistic corruptions. The various evils of caste have particularly arisen in recent social history.

Ramanujan says that the characteristic of Indian culture is to be recognized in the fact that it conceives of rules in a *contextual* manner. Thus, the discrimination between right and wrong, instead of being abstractly and absolutely formulated, is cast in terms of the given duties of one's caste or station. The model of Indian culture is *grammar* rather than *logic*. This suggestion is, doubtless, full of insight and is useful for understanding Indian social phenomena and rituals; but as an absolute categorization it cannot be regarded as an unconditional truth about Indian culture. Nor, indeed, can context-bound or context-free rules be isolated, just as the universal and the particular cannot be isolated. By the side of the relativity of empirical laws and values, one must seek their complement in the transcendental. The distinction between the context-free and context-bound is an important difference of cultural styles; but if the hierarchy of values are forgotten, it can be misleading.

Some contemporary sociologists and anthropologists tend to highlight the distinction between the *classical* and the *folk* dimension of Indian culture. This, however, proceeds from a mistaken belief, for the two dimensions have constituted one interacting tradition. The great leaders of Indian thought did not live a cloistered and isolated life. They lived the life of wandering *fakirs* talking to the people and speaking their language. Even the tradition of *Śāstras* have always been combined with actual practice, so that to understand the truth one need not be a learned man. The scientific *Śāstras* have remained alive and progressive.

The fact is that there is a tendency among the scholars to confuse the historical and sub-continental tradition of Indian culture with simply the surface phenomena of social life that vary from one another continually in space and time. Such an approach may be relevant to some extent for the anthropological study of pre-literate and ahistoric communities. It is totally inadequate for understanding Indian culture. What the external observer can see of Indian culture in behavioral terms is the tip of the iceberg. For culture, like man, has its essence in inward realization and not in external behavior, though behavior is relevant to the expression and realization of inward values.

It may be concluded that Indian culture is not a mere conglomerate of the diverse models and customs of the numberless communities that constitute India. It is not to be identified with contingent and ephemeral *lokavyavahāra*. It is a tradition of values claiming universal and perennial relevance (*sanātana dharma*). Originating in the interaction of diverse communities through the ages, Indian culture is a continental and catholic tradition that, in its essence, is not Indian in any restricted sense, but simply the Indian version of *philosophia perennis.*[1]

Note

1. For a detailed presentation of the views articulated above, see my *Foundations of Indian Culture: Spiritual Vision and Symbolic Forms in Ancient India*, Delhi, 1984.

10

On Tradition

A.K. SARAN

Epistle Dedicated to Bitta

> It is high time that some people turned their attention to the important problem of what constitutes an acceptable education in the Buddhist sense – the same applies to Hindus and indeed to all who have the spiritual welfare of their children at heart. Such persons should know that it is idle to aim at material benefits apart from the spiritual, for without the latter to give form and direction and meaning, there can be no true happiness and no contentment and no prosperity and no culture.
>
> Marco Pallis
> *The Way and the Mountain*

I have titled this address "On Tradition" rather than "Understanding Tradition". I take this liberty because the official title, "Understanding Tradition", already implies a certain view of

Tradition. It is one that emphasizes the conditions, the contexts, and the preconditions of understanding it.

Strangely enough, "understanding" – that is, the interpretation and presentation – of tradition has occurred in the context of modernity. This is plainly and inexplicably turning everything upside down, proceeding anachronistically and in the name of history. It is a view, a framework of analysis and understanding, which is accepted with willful enthusiasm by the (ex?) colonial people as a continuation of the universal white imperialism. Ours is a fate of flaunting perpetual slavery, of course, under cover of changing labels. For us, since 1947, it is Independence of our truncated bisected motherland, celebrated every year with great pomp and ceremony. We now celebrate universal white imperialism under the name (euphemism) of globalization.

The very context, the very pairing of modernity and tradition is anachronistic. Come modernity, tradition is annihilated – that much is clear, beyond doubt irrefutable. Where modernity is, to raise the question, whether tradition can also survive as something belonging partly or wholly to prehistory or to history? – then, naturally is to commit an obvious fallacy. Indeed, this is implied, though may not be immediately evident: the fallacy of anachronism.

Anachronization of history entails modernizing the past: a paradox with the force of self-contradiction. Understanding something in terms of ideas and things absent at the time in which the thing to be interpreted and understood is located – this is an anachronism: perhaps deliberately designed to give people a wrong picture of history on behalf of universal (and eternal) white imperialism. In fact, it is a device to destroy the very idea of tradition by shallow praise or by weak or strong criticism or whatever. In the synthesis syndrome of modernity and tradition, even with an understanding that is strongly critical, the object could not be to destroy that which is criticized. For if you destroy it, there is no need for criticism or any other weapon. But this is one of the worst weapons because it destroys: and yet for imperial purposes it keeps alive that which it has destroyed.

So I thought I would address you just "On Tradition". One ground precondition is quite obvious: that we should not pair it with modernity. It is not just a question of pairing, not one of putting it on the same plane as modernity. What one must see is that only when a thorough, penetrating and wholly destructive critique of modernity has been presented, could any talk of understanding modernity or tradition be meaningful. If you do not believe in any such precondition, then you want not to understand tradition, but simply to destroy it: by shallow praise or by loaded critiques.

Unlike most other concepts, that of *tradition* is not explicable in terms of distinction or contradistinction from any other concept or family of concepts. Above all – and this is of crucial importance – the concept of tradition has nothing whatsoever to do with modernity. Never mind, if it has always been so paired, not out of ignorance, but due to imperatives, the internal necessities of the theory and practice of modernity and modernization. These two are akin but not identical. The concepts are not really synonymous. The case I am pleading for is the cutting off of all relationship between tradition and modernity, putative or real (they are, in fact, just putative). But I do wish to emphasize that if you do so, you will have tremendous difficulty in explicating the concept of modernity. The first problem would be that then you cannot place modernity in history at all, it will become an ahistoric and atemporal concept that centrally and crucially contradicts modernity's self-definition.

Modernity's twin reigning goddesses are *history* on the one hand, and *science* on the other. History for modern man is chronology from an arbitrarily chosen "event", and science has no history, it is timeless. However, science has a history based on "the (total) conquest of nature (and man)" by man achieved for the ruling elite of the world – the elite that has to be the European white man – or so Husserl teaches.

Tradition *qua* tradition is timeless, but has multiple expressions, even if itself remaining Formless. Tradition cannot be understood by the method of difference nor by any kind of ostensive definition. It is sheer positivity and, paradoxically, the deepest and highest abstraction. Tradition as a concept or reality can be paired with no other word, concept or idea; nor can it be compared to any other kinds of reality. It is the bearer of the Non-manifest, of the Invisible, of the Incomprehensible, of the Inexpressible, of the Inexhaustible, that is, if such a tremendous burden can be borne at all by a single idea or concept. Without tradition, we will not *be*. Traditional thought, at another level, duplicates tradition. Thought is a trace, a first reification of thinking. Like tradition, thought too is man himself, the absolute, the divine, the void.

The essentials of traditional thought and civilization have been laid down by Marco Pallis in profound passages that are a "marvel" of beauty and verity:

> [1.] "... [B]y tradition more is meant than just custom long established, even if current usage has tended to restrict it in this way. Here the word will always be given its transcendent, which is also its normal, connotation without any attempt being made, however, to pin it down to a particular set of concepts, if only because tradition, being formless and suprapersonal in its essence, escapes exact definition in terms of human speech or thought. All that can usefully be said of it at the moment is that wherever a complete tradition exists this will entail the presence of four

things, namely: a source of inspiration or, to use a more concrete term, of Revelation; a current of influence or Grace issuing forth from that source and transmitted without interruption through a variety of channels; a way of "verification" which, when faithfully followed, will lead the human subject to successive positions where he is able to "actualize" the truths that Revelation communicates; finally there is the formal embodiment of tradition in the doctrines, arts, sciences and other elements that together go to determine the character of a normal civilization."

[2.] "A traditional civilization has its roots set in a doctrine of the purely metaphysical order, from which all the other constituents of the tradition, whether ethical, social or artistic down to the most petty activities of daily life derive their sanction. Metaphysical ideas are the cement that binds every part together. The whole body of thought and action must be viewed as a hierarchy, with pure metaphysics at the head."

[3.] "One essential means whereby the truth is made to circulate among men is the tradition from Master to pupil, which stretches back into the past and reaches forward to the future. By the doctrine so handed down, all parts are related to one another; they derive from it both stability and elasticity. No set of boundaries can be recognized by Tradition as such; it can only be taken as the mobile vehicle of graces in fact unchanging."

My original idea was to take the four essentials of the existence and continuance of a normal civilization (mentioned in the first passage) one by one. But that would mean a three or four times longer presentation than the present one. So I will only comment on one or two, my basic text being the one I quoted from Marco Pallis.

Today one scarcely needs to go into the rather complex, if not complicated, relationship between tradition and custom.

Marco Pallis has laid down one negative and four positive conditions for the existence, sustenance and continuity of civilization and traditional society. The negative condition is this: Custom is intimately related to tradition. In one sense, the relation could even be seen as principal. Even so, tradition is not just custom long established. I come now directly to the situation of tradition in contemporary times: the problem of relating or understanding the relation between custom and tradition in one way or another is not however obsolete today. Indeed, it has been so for close to a century, but we have been trying to be deaf to the voices prophesying doom. That is, we thought that custom is something that we have now superseded; that we can and do live now by rationality – except in the situation where rationality grows into a custom yet retaining its rationality; and that modernity has achieved this combination of rationality and custom for its continuance. Because of this, we think, we no longer deal with custom either on a praxiological plane or on a purely theoretical plane. The problem is already solved.

However, we ignore the astounding, penetrating and profound message of Nietzsche, who died at the beginning of the 20th century, exactly in 1900. But the 20th century needs to listen, to pay heed to his message more than did the 19th century. The problems that could only be foreseen by prophets are now everyday problems, however ignored or disguised or papered over or whatever. He says: "people have no notion yet that from now onwards (i.e., from the last quarter of the 19th century if not earlier) they exist on the mere pittance of inherited and decaying values", soon only to be overtaken by an enormous bankruptcy, as Erich Heller despairingly commented.[4] Now, may I draw your attention to this doubly, trebly, or even infinitely potential phrase: "the pittance of inherited and decaying values". These inherited values fail us today: even insofar as we recognize them as pittance, a pittance presumably to save us against the realization, the awareness, of our enormous bankruptcy. Once we stop ignoring and begin to be conscious of the burden of the enormous bankruptcy we face today, the contemporaneity of tradition and the obsolescence of modernity will be utterly obvious.

Now, tradition is *formless, transcendental* and *supra-personal.* Hence, it is beyond any exact definition in terms of human speech or thought. At the same time, it must be made clear that tradition is by no means a humanistic or sociological category. It is at once a human and a trans-human category: a sort of anthropo-metaphysical idea and reality. That is to say, the meaning of human life and the meaning of tradition go together. However, in the sense in which man is dependent on tradition, tradition is not dependent on man; it is not man who gives meaning to tradition. It is from tradition that man's life and history derive their meaning and purpose. However, the context of tradition is man. Elucidation of the concept of tradition is immediately related to the question of human nature and of human essence. Man, insofar as he is a man, is not real, for the Real is that which is absolutely self-existing and self-subsisting and remains what it is *in itself.* But man is a composite of many things and does not remain such as he is in himself, but shifts and changes from one age to another and from one form to another. The criterion of reality, not that of permanence but of identity is certainly presupposed in this traditional denial of man's reality.

Man, therefore, could think that there is no logical obligation to accept this criterion. It is doubtful if any definition of reality could violate or neglect the notion of self-identity. However, we need not entertain that question here: the essential fact of human mortality is undeniable. To admit this is to admit that man has no self-grounded, self-sufficient reality. Or to put it differently, so as to avoid the question of a presupposed criterion of reality, man's reality and nature must proceed from the truth that he is not self-grounded, and that he is the being that can and must ask the reflexive-ontological question: Who am I? Now, this question is in no sense the meaningless anthropological question: what is man? Nor would it do to ask, who is man? For to the irrefutably legitimate question: who is asking? there can be no answer that could avoid the tautological implication, the implication that at once renders the question (who, or what, man?) is inconsistent if not strictly meaningless. Here, it is supposed that the reality of the questioner and the reality of the question are identical. Thus, to suppose that man could at all ask, what is man?, from a standpoint outside of anthropology, beyond the human pale, is plainly absurd. Then, *who* is this questioner? Is he the ethnographer, the ethnologist, the anthropologist? When man is questioning his own self, it must be in the first person, it cannot be in the third person. But then modern social science will not be possible unless we postulate the strange phantom in which the observer and the observed are one, but also absolutely disparate – and not relatively, because we cannot define the relative. Except you could find no fault with this strange phantom that you feel familiar with it – this ghost from nowhere. No, you cannot at all entertain this "question": what is man? I do not know how it has been entertained at all, retained so long. Indeed I am afraid that this pseudo and sinister "question" will continue to be asked and answered no matter how many times and how many people come and try to let you see the absurdity of it.

It is clear that the ontological question does not avoid the problem of self-reflexivity of human consciousness and *noesis*; indeed, it intensifies it. It is admitted that the individuality of the fundamental human condition is the result of defining man in terms of language. If one drops the linguistic context, reflexivity ceases to be the original nature of man – in any case, not axiomatically.

Now in order to decide whether it makes sense to drop the linguistic context – that is to say, if it is possible at all to imagine (even though not to define), logico-dialectically or existentially, "man" (that is, we ourselves) without some kind of language – a brief clarification of the notion of language is necessary.

Firstly, we are not concerned here with the communicative or the exhibitive use of language; it is not its primary or essential use. I am referring here to the famous and fundamental distinction made by Coomaraswamy among others.[5] The exhibitive use of language is to show oneself: in an egocentric, non-meaningful, self-indexical mode or auto-idolatrous way – bordering on the idiopathic. (The exhibitive is eventually the idiotic.) The communicative use of language, on the other hand, renders a meaning through iconic, indexical and symbolic modes. It is to use language in order ultimately to suggest a trans-human, trans-personal, trans-mundane reality. The communicative use of language is thus teleologically ordered. The exhibitive is univocal, whereas the communicative is multivocal; the former opaque, the latter transparent. In other words, in the exhibitive use, the medium is the message (full stop). In the communicative use, the message is conveyed through the self-cancelling of the medium. What Coomaraswamy suggests is something drastic, almost unbelievable, that modern man is reduced to using language exhibitively, unmindful of or spurning all its contradictions and literal, unmeaning paradoxes. Tradition is based on the communicative use of language, not only in the sense of inter-personal communication, but, more importantly, in the sense of communicating a trans-personal, trans-human reality. This alone is the purpose of human language and life. If language could not or did not go beyond serving as a means of communication between persons, then the exhibiting, instead of myself, becomes that of a 'collectivity.'

In truth, the essential, principal use of language is recreative, reintegrative and revelatory. It is this that is implied by the fact that even to imagine (say, in the manner of a "thought experiment") a state of affair when man existentially was, or must have been, mute (or deaf and mute) is impossible. To see this with the finality theorems demand, it is necessary further to clarify the notion of language in *principio*, in *theoria*; it would be a necessary (though not a sufficient) condition to have access to a general theory of Language – one that combines with near universal reach and the deepest grasp, say, one that could embrace Egyptian hieroglyphs ("pictographs"), Chinese "ideograms", Sanskrit "alphabet" at its highest level. One wonders if this ambition could ever be actually realized, if such an "ideal" (or, should one say, "ideational", ideogrammatic) language could ever function for the non-initiated scholar.

At this level, the distinction between the communicative and exhibitive uses of language would not operate. In other words, this is my long and rather jumbled way of suggesting the right method to handle the problematics here, namely, Bhartṛhari's fourfold hierarchical classification of language (in his *Vākyapadiya*): the absolutely transcendental, *Parā*; the intuitively luminous, *Paśyantī*, the metaphorical-figurative, *Madhyamā*; and, the literal, articulative, *Vaikhārī*.[6] On this plane, Coomaraswamy's distinction between the communicative and exhibitive uses of language has to be transcended in order to realize that figures of *speech* are figures of *thought*.

Parā is the supreme, the utterly Dark background of all manifestation. It is the void: the atemporal. In Gopinath Kaviraj's immaculate description, *paśyantī* is the backshining of *parā*.[7] Even the *pasyanti* level is beyond man; it is trans-human. Man is confined only to *madhyamā* and *vaikhārī*. But man can, in his outer (and higher) reaches, touch the *paśyantī*, but not *parā*. *Parā* is necessary as a concept because otherwise *paśyantī* will not get any meaning or background at all. And then, consequently, even *madhyamā* and *vaikhārī* will be baseless. *Paśyantī* is eternal. The intuitively luminous is eternally undivided, non-successive and syntaxless. This is the linguistic level that is subtle and supra-sensuous and is the source of all knowledge. Articulate language or *vaikhārī* is at the lowest level in this hierarchy and normally man has access to articulate language only. Yogis can have access to *madhyamā* and *paśyantī*.

In this sense of articulate language, it is certainly possible to drop the assumption of linguisticality in the conceptualization of man. But now we should remember that reflexivity, as we usually understand it, reflexivity in the articulate *vaikhārī* level of language, is – that is, after all, any manifestation in any mode at any level (including *madhyamā*) – a rupture of the primordial unity that is Non-manifest. The possibility inherent in the act of creation and of reintegration is the essential meaning of reflexivity. I mean something very simple and something quite well-known – that human consciousness is so structured, and it functions in such a way, that any cognition at any level becomes the object of another consciousness. So from that point of view, every consciousness is reflexively reproduced, not originally but to reproduce itself or function by reproducing itself. All cognition is housed in a previous cognition. This is an infinite chain. And that is why I used "self-reflexivity" rather than "reflexivity", of consciousness, especially cognition.

I was talking about the act of creation, the creationist perspective. It is the cosmological perspective that posits a timeless, eternal centre of manifestation and copes with time by transcending it rather than by conquering it; the latter is a falsification of time. The flowing character of time is preserved, but this flow, by virtue of the origin in an eternal centre, has an outward and an inward, a forward and a backward direction. Tradition is the name of the relation of man to the eternal center.

But this relation between the eternal centre and the flows of manifestation and non-manifestation is a mystery. Hence, strictly speaking, tradition is nameless, indefinable, beyond thought like the eternal centre, the void, the *Parabrahma*. It is not identical with the centre, but is mysteriously related to the centre from which it flows and to which it returns. Again, like the centre, tradition is one but it is manifested in the order of manyness.

The metaphysical in its nature and its externalization in religion benefits all of us; its highest modality is what reality is for all of us at whatever level. Modernization is some kind of religion whether you convert to it or resist it. Religion has to be grounded in a theology, but a theology without metaphysics is inconceivable.

The whole idea of tradition is bound up with the doctrine that man is Self and has a *self* that he is *not*. In the sense in which he is his higher *Self*, he is *not* his lower self. The lower self has to be transcended and become identical with the higher Self. The duality has to be transcended. Our whole metaphysical tradition maintains that there are the two in us. This man and the Man'in this man. This is part and parcel of our spoken language in which, for example, the expression 'self-control' implies that there are two in us: the One that controls and the other that is subject to control.

We know that nothing acts upon itself. Even so we forget just that when we talk of self-government, of the outer and the inner man, and psycho-physical personality. The mutable and the mortal is the lower self, the self that is controlled: we say "self-control", "being self-assured" or "self-confident", "losing yourself', or "losing your temper" and so on. The temper that is lost must also be my own. This duality is not contingent but necessary to all communication, indeed to all thinking. Except in the higher stages of *samādhi*, which we cannot talk about here, these dualities remain. The one *is* and the other *becomes*. The existence of one that is *not* but *becomes* is precisely a personification, because originally the person is that through (*per*) which one sound speaks out (*sono*): one's action and the response to the others' actions. It is a dramaturgic term because originally drama was the reenactment of what the Gods did before (archetypes). A person is one who personates that which he is not: he is what he has to become. All action is thus impersonation, the negativity (morality-immorality) of which has to be redeemed by inner dissociation from one's act. Action is the fruit of the oratorical: only apparently the consequence of previous action. So it is essential for any drama, any acting, that the actor speaks. Speech and drama go together. Acting, even miming, would not be conceivable without implicit speech.

Human reflexivity implies that there are the two in us: the transcendent Self and the spatio-temporal self. Given man's reflexivity, logically, dialectically, existentially, the very idea of "world view" is, at best, dubious: this idea (world view or world picture) has been shown by Heidegger decisively – and I hope, once for all – to be the *entelechic* constitution of modern age aided and abetted by man's oblivion of Being. Otherwise "it would have to confess itself shaken and overcome"[8] It is high time we adjusted ourselves to its profound implications.

To understand the doctrine of two selves is to see that man's humanity and, hence his dignity, is to strive towards the higher, transcendent Self. Because, if you don't cultivate, ultimately and almost exclusively, the controlling Self, you are allowing yourself to be the prisoner of multiple selves. We are practising self-betrayal – and, indeed, in every sense of the word.

To understand the doctrine of two selves is to see that man's humanity and, hence his dignity, is naturally axiomatically towards the higher transcendent Self. It just cannot be otherwise; all other possibilities are closed. I cannot descend to the lower self. I cannot remain, stay put at the middle level: that will cancel the series; that is, I would have already transcended time. It follows that I can only make an ascent to the higher Self. Or not. Even so I would have to ignore my destiny. The decisive thing is this: the question of destiny or meaning of life does not arise at all if I am nothing but a part of the phenomenal flow. I am not only a part of this flow. I can stand apart from it, look back upon myself and my lived time. And if this act is real, then my transcendent Self too is real.

Man's "Evolution" and History are contradicted by his self-reflexive consciousness. Tradition represents to me this Transcendent consciousness at the conjuncture of time and eternity. Indeed I could go so far as to suggest that to say that 'I am' cannot but be to say that I am before all my intelligence and Intellect. Also I am wisdom and contemplation. And by further consequence, I *am* Tradition which possesses me and with which I have to be at-one. To detach myself from the Tradition is to render myself "independent": hanging loose, deprived of my divine-humanity, existing miscellaneously.

Conversely, to deny Tradition is to deny the intellectual transcendent Self – *the Man in man* – a denial that perforce imprisons me in the constant flow of phenomena. Our limited powers and virtually unlimited wants *ex hypothesi* invest me with an indefinitely extended imprisonment. Indeed, I am worse off. My wants and ambitions require me to outstretch my powers. This I cannot, since I refuse and reject the higher *telos*, relation to which my continual efforts to break the bounds unmistakably point. But, then, is not Tradition itself, the transcendence that it represents, a project of my mind, one of the myriad illusory devices to escape time, to burst its bonds? This can be brought as an objection to this analysis. The true and brief answer and also the traditional one is: Yes, indeed it is. But this must be understood and verified with one's whole being. One who proposes to cross a river needs a boat (that is, if he cannot swim over to the other shore). But when one has already arrived, one no longer needs a boat. It is left on the shore.

Revelation itself implies a vision rather than a disclosure, a symbol and a mystery rather than a sign, a means of communication. It is half-revealed-half-concealed and it aptly describes the parabolic style of the Scriptures. The scriptures are conceptual images of Being-in-Itself which cannot disclose Itself to our physical senses. And so, it is said by one of the *Upanisads* that the highest wisdom or knowledge taught by the *Upanisads* themselves is the last form of *avidyā*, ignorance.

Now man is Tradition. Yes, but this does not reduce Tradition to man but identifies him with it. The objection that all this is a projection, an opium devised by the Capitalist for exploiting the proletariat, has been answered above. Indeed, logically it is an irrelevant and incompetent question, the question, namely, whether the Other Shore and human *askesis* to seek it is an illusion, an opium of mankind or man's consciousness overlaid by false, ideological consciousness – all these are modern devices to perpetuate white Western global imperialism. But, strictly, logically, it is an irrelevant and an incompetent question: that Tradition is a projection of man implies that Man himself is his own projection. We are back to infinite self-reflexivity of our consciousness and the dialectically implicated Transcendence with which we started. For any Marxist, the challenge is to honestly, and consistently, explain how the consciousness of man comes to be falsified. How so? If it becomes false by human determination, then it is not false but a forged one. What then could be the argument, the logic that would guarantee the truth of false consciousness? Society would then either determine man according to a formula laid down once for all by some prophet, or it would not determine man at all, and yet be related to man, will yet be human society and not something independent of man.

Tradition belongs to the twilight space-time between man and the absolute reality or Void or Godhead. It is twilight between time and Eternity. It is not man or time except as man who has realized his Self. It is always man and time, man in time but in the time that is the backshining of Eternity. At the same time, tradition is not Eternity, the Absolute, the Real, the Void or Godhead. In itself, the Absolute admits of no mediator whatsoever and can be suggested only *via negativa,* that is, *neti neti,* It is not this. I said it is sheer positivity. And then it is clear why the *via negativa* is identical with positivity in the sense that the *neti* denied is not 'something but whatever might be positive'.

Tradition is therefore absolute reality. The Godhead is one. Godhead here implies the Eckhartian distinction between God and Godhead. Godhead as the *Nirguṇa* distinguished from the *saguṇa Īśvara*. The forms and vehicles of expression are many and manifold. The forms are divergent: sometimes even conflicting. All these forms and vehicles of expression are manifestations, suggestions of the One Tradition *via affirmativa.* The ultimate meaning of these suggestions is *via negativa*: by negating them (suggestions) you reach something. But then it is not anything.

The One Tradition of which all traditions are varied expressions: what is its nature? An answer to this is imperative before attempting an answer to the question, what the nature of expressed traditions is.

About the One Tradition the Pallis text says: "being formless and supra-personal in its essence, It escapes exact definition in terms of human speech and thought." The distinction between the effable and the ineffable, the thinkable and the unthinkable, knowing and unknowing, mentation and de-mentation, *via affirmativa* and *via negativa* has always been made. This is simply unavoidable, implicit in man's self-reflexivity: the fact that one consciousness is always the object of another consciousness or cognition.

We are not concerned here with the paradoxes of heterologicality. The paradox is the deeper intimation of that which transcends language and thought. This is the paradox, the Mystery of language. That is why a modern author, R.A. Wilson names his treatise on language *The Miraculous Birth of Language.* How is this possible? No attempt will be made here to explicate the mystery of Language. Only some elucidation, some suggestions towards approaching this central mystery (of Creation) may be essayed here.

All uses of language from the simplest and the most trivial to the complicated and the profoundest show the mysterious power of language and its esoterism. Through language man can talk about what he has not experienced and thus participate in the birth of a lie. The falsifying power of language is co-eval with the origin of language. It does not say anything about the Primordial Word. It has been very often remarked that language is the mother of both truth and falsehood: a non-linguistic communication or creation cannot speak a lie, though, of course, there could be mythical forms of wordless temptation. This constitutes the mystery that true and false are nothing if not diametrically opposed to each other. In any given situation it may be a half lie or a quarter lie or a half-truth or near-truth. In any logical analysis, a truth is a truth is a truth and a lie is a lie is a lie. The *Mysterium Magnum* is that Language mothers both (we do not know the father).

Language is not just a generalized means of communication or even a system for organizing our experience and imagination etc. We mean, by language, any system through which man relates himself to himself, to other men, to his environment and, in the last analysis, to the supra-human in a transcending elucidatory mode. Or else, all other relationships will become inexplicable. It derives its operative power from its cosmological matrix. That leads to a journey to chaos-cosmos-chaos: a journey prohibited to this side of sainthood.

If language can suggest, and in some way express, the Whole, that in some way can be transcended. If you at all distinguish between an aggregate and a whole, then language is ultimately cosmological. However, the specificity of this linguistic relation is its revealing, transcending power. All relationship between man and the other, nature or any other reality, as also to his own self (and Self), is in terms of the other as a series, x and y, a or b. The object of relation has to be seen as this or that; or no specific relationship can be founded. It then reveals another – and in most cases myself – as thus and so; that which is just *suchness*. It is that which constitutes the power to generalize. Generalization is inherent in language: impossible non-linguistically. To illustrate this in terms of ordinary verbal communication: even when we do not know the person who is encountering us or whom we are encountering, we call him a stranger. And perhaps the word "stranger" reveals an aspect of his being, as well as a world shared in common by us, and it is this that generates a relationship. I mean, on the one hand, a stranger is one to whom we are not related or could possibly get related, but not yet: but the word indicates already a relationship and not just an indefinite possibility of a relationship. When, later, he is made a friend, another revelation has taken place through the assertion of the word "friend", through the positivity of the word "friend" and negativity of the word "stranger". Every word is part of a language-system, and within it part of a specific family of words: the relationship is interpreted, developed, analyzed. It could, of course, mature even without these operations through the concepts that form the family of the original revelatory Word.

The constellation of thoughts and feelings that forms around a revelation, if it could be understood, clarified, grasped, it would be only through linguistic conceptual thinking. Now transcending my relation to myself and to the universe is at once expansive and limiting. The two movements are incompatible. Two different possibilities are entailed. One: all relations are unreal and hence must be negated. Two: that since the relations do exist on a certain plane of reality, the essence of the relations must be outside the two movements. We may see it as only expansive or as only limiting; or as both. In all the three cases, a relationship reveals the parties *ex hypothesi* as limited beings. The more tense the relationship of limitedness, the keener is the urge to transcend the relationship in a movement towards wholeness. Let us remember that the *holy* and the *whole* are precisely the same in meaning as well as in etymology. In "whole", "w" has come to be added as an anglicization of originally a Greek word; the W-H-O-L-E is the Holy: the H-O-L-Y, the Sacred.

Now, from another perspective also we arrive at, essentially, the same point. Man is necessarily involved in a chain of relationships with his universe, some of which have a specific purpose and can be seen in a framework of instrumental, contractual or any other type of classification. Others have no specific end and do not fit into a means-end framework. The latter clearly involves a transcendence of the specificity of the relationship and an underlying orientation to an absolute *telos*. Now the instrumental and contractual relationships can only be held together in terms of the ultimate ends of man's life, spiritual and secular. In view of this, each specific relationship has to be transcended in a movement towards a higher and more encompassing relationship. I say this to refute the idea that the instrumental and the contractual can constitute an independent sphere. What I mean is that it is not at all a kind of typology of action. Traditional vision of life refutes, once for all, the Parsonsian theory of action. Tradition enables man to be aware of the opacity-transparency of all his relations; it is what saves him from the deadening momentariness of all his experience, events, relationships, and enables him to see them as symbols suggesting higher realities, and thereby, makes it possible for him to transcend them.

Now our decision to stick to the term *language* and language-systems, while giving it a most generalized, almost universal, meaning and reference, could cause some confusion. It is sometimes forgotten that the spoken and written language is only one kind of language, even though it has a unique importance in the life of man. Indeed, our use of the term "language" covers different types of languages operating on other planes of reference. Forms of expression in different arts, say, the language of drama, the language of sculpture and painting, are different from vocalizable languages, and their translation back into something that can be vocalized cannot but miss the essence. There must be a direct relationship to such languages.

The above analysis seeks to show that the whole of man's relationship to his universe is linguistic or symbolic in the above sense of the term. There is an important aspect of meaning in which there is nothing that is human and *not* linguistic or symbolic. It may seem a trivial statement.

It should be pointed out that we have mentioned three marks of human language or forms of expression: revelatory, elucidatory and transcending. This makes all relationship linguistic in a three-fold form. It may still be objected that the three marks of a linguistic relationship, describe at the same time the phenomenology of human relationships and thus indirectly make all human relations linguistic. If our phenomenology of human relations is sound, then it tells us about man and the universe something that, far from being trivial, is of the greatest importance. In the second place, and at a lower level, the universality of language is limited by the ever-present possibility of the obscuration in the functioning of a specific system. There thus arise non-linguistic, non-symbolic, scientific or empirical "human" relationships.

Let me now consider this possibility. Take the technological or the instrumental order: an airplane, a hammer – or a fountain pen. Are these parts of the language system in the general or the specific sense? In a specific sense, language is any system of signs for the purposes of communication of messages between two or more entities, a sign being any fact standing for another – a sensible fact. Now it could seem that a pen or a hammer is not necessarily part of a language system in the general sense of the term: neither fulfils the three conditions of revelation, elucidation and transcendence. Indeed, it may also seem that nothing in the technological-instrumental order satisfies any definition of language in the non-figurative, non-reflexive terms. The hammer, the airplane, the fountain pen are not signs, nor do they convey any message. They are just instruments. They get a certain job done when used properly. Of course, physically and linguistically, each can be used both as a sign and a symbol (e.g. Cartier Gold Fountain Pen).

But there are difficulties. For instance, in the cybernetic sense, and in the sense of information theory, the whole of the instrumental-technic order is seen as a communication system. Cybernetics will make all kinds of relationships part of a communicative or auto-communicative system. Waiving all such difficulties for the moment, let us treat the instrumental order as an independent, non-linguistic one. Fundamental problems arise here. One has already been suggested: Does not the instrumental order presuppose language in the sense in which logic and mathematics are systems of special languages? I will not raise, at this stage, the question whether their relation to ordinary verbal language is contingent or necessary. The language of mathematics (especially algebra), symbolic logic, computer systems or other kinds of cybernetic systems is one that is dominated by syntactics: thus non-human. Indeed one could say that they are purely syntactical – without any semantics. In the Charles Morris classification of human communication as syntactics, semantics and pragmatics, the continuity between the first two and the third remains unresolved. A moderately complex instrumental order would be impossible without some development of mathematical languages. The worlds of nature, of history must already stand in a certain relationship to man before an appropriate instrumental order can develop. This, however, does not prove that the instrumental is linguistic in any of the two senses. Our argument shows only this: it is not independent of the language order. One could ask: why cannot we regard the instrumental order itself as the first order relation between man and nature? The linguistic orders in any sense of the term may then be derived from the instrumental order. There are indeed instrumental theories of language: biotechnic, psychotechnic and purely technological theories and cybernetic and information theories generalized to function as a general theory of language.

It is clear, I suppose, that any instrumental theory of language entails an instrumental theory of man. It can be an anthropology of *homo faber*. But we have shown throughout this presentation that this does not and cannot make sense. It is based on a false anthropology. Man is distinguished from the rest of creation by the fact that he is part of the natural world and yet stands, in a preeminent way, apart from it. One crucial aspect of this distinction is his self-reflexivity. I rejected anthropology on this very ground. It is impossible that he could have a need-based, immediate but eventually exploitative, relationship with the natural world. Even if that were possible, the relation is bound to be exploitative and therefore self-destructive. Our argument is this: there is a discontinuity between the need-centred animal man not implying the existence of any supra-human being, and the reflexive, rational, intellectual-spiritual and whole man. The whole man must first have a holistic, that is, wholesome, relationship to nature in terms of which alone his needs will find meaning and satisfaction. Otherwise, he will be, ultimately and teleologically, a person defined as one, who has needs, and therefore, creates need-satisfying systems. Again, this entails the actuality, independently of its possibility, of an intelligent being, who systematically aims to destroy his own support-system.

Earlier, we posited the existence of a linguistic support system between man and the universe that had three marks: revelation, elucidation and transcendence. That there are such relationships cannot be denied. To grant this leaves one with three possibilities: a duality of what in sociology-jargon is called the *expressive* and the *instrumental* orders; secondly, the expressive is reduced to the instrumental; and thirdly, the instrumental is reduced to the expressive. It could be objected to the first, that the expressive and the instrumental remain sundered from each other, unless an internal relation can be shown between the two. This kind of relation cannot be made to fit in any schema in which all kinds of instrumental relations must fit. The linguistic relationship is essentially reintegrative. The basic *apūrṇess* of man that is presupposed in any human relationship is integrated back in the primordial unity that is postulated in all cosmological perspectives. The instrumental relationship cannot take on any such role. By its very nature, it presupposes apartness, the separateness of man and nature. It is true that technological relationships, instrumentalism, rationalism, and science can and do build bridges between man and nature. They create new relationships, but that is clearly a different matter. This leads to another point. Instrumental relationships are finite relationships and the instrument can do only a finite number of jobs. In a language-system, even a single word has an infinite reference and meaning with the possibilities of being used in a multidimensional manner. As soon as we have an instrument in terms of its purpose, use and impact at different levels, we are already treating technology or the instrumental order. A language-system, with all the implications, all the expressibility and the inexpressibility, communicates the communicable, and paradoxically communicates also the incommunicable.

Now, how is linguistic relation possible? Whether we ask this question in a general sense or specifically in a verbal sense, the problem remains. Language refers to reality. Language as the vehicle or sign may refer to reality on the same plane or on a different discontinuous plane. In each case, the sign is seen both as a fact and transparently not as itself, but as a relationship between two discontinuous planes. There is this central mystery of the sign that is both a sign and a non-sign. And this is essential to its being. It abolishes itself in the very act of pointing. If you then see the moon, however beautiful the finger pointing to it is, then you must negate the pointing finger. Without the self-negation of the sign, no signifying function is possible. The sign functions transparently, not as itself, but as the signified, even though the relationship between the two remains, in important senses, discontinuous. Here we encounter the mystery of the sign: it is a sign and not a sign – almost in the same breath.

Language as a vehicle of thought and conceptualization presents to us the mystery of incommensurability (between the tangible or even the intangible vehicle of thought and the concepts to which they refer.) We face an undeniable continuity as well as depths of discontinuity. In the most general sense of the terms, language *sans* thought and reality stand on incommensurate planes. Even so, neither is intelligible without the other. What of the category "intelligibility" itself? Intelligibility implicates the incommensurate planes of language *sans* thought and reality.

This means that a theory of man must at the same time be a theory of language. And a theory of language must at the same time be a theory of man, and both must imply a supra-linguistic and trans-human Reality. It is from this supra-linguistic and trans-human Reality that language and man as its implicates get the powers of expression, action, self-reflexivity that are essential to them. The higher Self and the lower self are, and operate, in continuous relation in spite of their inviolable discontinuity.

Tradition implies a theory of Being and a theory of Man's Becoming. It is the essentiality of the chasm between becoming and Being that commands our *askesis* towards unity in the timeless: an *askesis* which cannot begin *sans* Tradition ever and everywhere given to us from Above.

Notes

1. Pallis, Marco, *The Way and the Mountain*, New Delhi, 1994, pp. 9-10.
2. ibid.
3. Marco Pallis, *Peaks and Lamas*, London, 1974, pp. xiv-xv.
4. Quoted and commented by Erich Heller in his, *The Artist's Journey into the Interior and Other Essays*, New York, 1968, p. 170. Parenthesis added.

5. See A.K. Coomaraswamy, *Myth and Meaning*, New Jersey, 1985.
6. See K.A. Subramania Iyer, *Bhartrhari: A Study of Vakyapadiya in the Light of Ancient Commentaries*, Poona, 1969.
7. Kaviraj, Gopinath, *Aspects of Indian Thought*, Burdwan, 1966, p. 19.
8. Heidegger, Martin, *The Question Concerning Technology and Other Essays*, New York, 1977, pp. 115-154.

Index